Designs for Learning

Organisation for Economic Co-operation and Development

Pursuant to Article 1 of the Convention signed in Paris on 14th December 1960, and which came into force on 30th September 1961, the Organisation for Economic Co-operation and Development (OECD) shall promote policies designed:

- to achieve the highest sustainable economic growth and employment and a rising standard of living in Member countries, while maintaining financial stability, and thus to contribute to the development of the world economy;

- to contribute to sound economic expansion in Member as well as non-member countries in the process of economic development; and

- to contribute to the expansion of world trade on a multilateral, non-discriminatory basis in accordance with international obligations.

The original Member countries of the OECD are Austria, Belgium, Canada, Denmark, France, Germany, Greece, Iceland, Ireland, Italy, Luxembourg, the Netherlands, Norway, Portugal, Spain, Sweden, Switzerland, Turkey, the United Kingdom and the United States. The following countries became Members subsequently through accession at the dates indicated hereafter: Japan (28th April 1964), Finland (28th January 1969), Australia (7th June 1971), New Zealand (29th May 1973), Mexico (18th May 1994), the Czech Republic (21st December 1995), Hungary (7th May 1996), Poland (22nd November 1996), Korea (12th December 1996) and the Slovak Republic (14th December 2000). The Commission of the European Communities takes part in the work of the OECD (Article 13 of the OECD Convention).

Publié en français sous le titre:
ARCHITECTURE ET APPRENTISSAGE : 55 ÉTABLISSEMENTS D'ENSEIGNEMENT EXEMPLAIRES

Designs for Learning: 55 Exemplary Educational Facilities is about the contribution that high-quality buildings can make to the educational process. Through examples from across the world, it demonstrates how the design, use and management of buildings and grounds improve teaching and learning.

Ninety schools and universities from 21 OECD countries submitted newly built or renovated facilities illustrating themes including schools in the information society, educational facilities and the environment, libraries and learning resource centres, as well as the design of institutions for the early years of tertiary education, and health, safety and security. This book follows the successful first PEB compendium, *Schools for Today and Tomorrow* published in 1996. That volume was devoted specifically to primary and secondary school facilities; this second compendium also includes tertiary institutions (universities, colleges and other post-secondary institutions) and facilities for adult education.

An international jury composed of people with backgrounds in architecture, education and resource allocation for school buildings made the final selection of facilities. The 55 institutions featured in this publication were judged to best demonstrate quality in one or more of the categories addressed by PEB in its 1997-2001 mandate. The jury wished to distinguish a small number of facilities they considered particularly remarkable; these are presented in Chapter 1.

The PEB Steering Committee wishes to sincerely thank all those who participated in this project, and in particular the jury.

Also available

The Appraisal of Investments in Educational Facilities, 1999, 236 pages, ISBN 92-64-17036-7, OECD code: 95 2000 01 1P	FRF 150	USD 24	DEM 45	GB£ 15	JPY 2,600
Garantire un ambiente sicuro per la scuola/Cómo garantizar un entorno seguro para la enseñanza, 1999, bilingual, 84 pages, ISBN 92-64-45756-9, OECD code: 95 98 01 4P	FRF 110	USD 19	DEM 33	GBP 11	JPY 2,350
Providing a Secure Environment for Learning/Assurer la sécurité du milieu éducatif, 1998, bilingual, 84 pages, ISBN 92-64-05756-0, OECD code: 95 98 01 3P	FRF 110	USD 19	DEM 33	GBP 11	JPY 2,350
Facilities for Tertiary Education in the 21st Century, 1998, 92 pages, ISBN 92-64-16081-7, OECD code: 95 98 02 1P	FRF 70	USD 12	DEM 20	GBP 7	JPY 1,500

"PEB Papers" series

Strategic Asset Management for Tertiary Institutions, 1999, 72 pages, ISBN 92-64-17014-6, OECD code: 95 99 01 1P	FRF 140	USD 25	DEM 42	GBP 15	JPY 3,150
Under One Roof - The Integration of Schools and Community Services in OECD Countries, 1998, 65 pages, ISBN 92-64-16110-4, OECD code: 95 98 03 1P	FRF 120	USD 20	DEM 36	GBP 12	JPY 2,550
Making Better Use of School Buildings, 1996, 40 pages, ISBN 92-64-14880-9, OECD code: 95 96 04 1P	FRF 60	USD 12	DEM 17	GBP 8	JPY 1,380
Schools for Today and Tomorrow, 1996, 130 pages, ISBN 92-64-15291-1, OECD code: 95 96 05 1P	FRF 200	USD 40	DEM 60	GBP 26	JPY 4,200

Periodical

PEB Exchange, (three issues per year), ISSN 1018-9327, OECD code: 88 00 00 1P	FRF 290	USD 55	DEM 95	GBP 31	JPY 5,900

To order:

DVG mbH (OECD)
Birkenmaarstrasse 8
D-53340 Meckenheim
Germany
Tel.: 49 22 25 9 26 166 to 168
Fax: 49 22 25 9 26 169

OECD Online Bookshop
http://www.oecd.org/bookshop/

Chapter Three: Tertiary Education – Coping with Demand

Chapter Four: Strategies for Managing the Educational Infrastructure

The challenge of change

We live in an era of rapidly accelerating social, economic and technical change. Many aspects of change in the field of education affect the design of schools, colleges and universities. Existing educational buildings and tried and tested approaches for new building are no longer appropriate to the new needs. The new demands call for new solutions.

In selecting the projects for inclusion in this compendium, the jury looked for schools and universities that demonstrate original and imaginative responses to these new challenges.

Criteria for selection

Educational facilities need to accommodate both the known and identifiable needs of today, and the uncertain demands of the future. They should provide an environment that will support and enhance the learning process, encourage innovation and be a tool for learning and not a monument to aesthetics. They need to be conceived not as an exclusive provision for the few, but as a resource to support lifelong education and recreation for all. They should provide good value for money. They should seek to minimise running and maintenance costs, ensuring that today's design decisions do not impose an unnecessary burden on future generations. Finally, they need to be designed to safeguard the wellbeing of the planet as well as the wellbeing of the individual.

In addition to these practical considerations, the jury looked for projects which provide that essential and elusive quality of delight. Delight that stems from the relationship of the buildings to the surrounding environment, from the choice of materials, from form and proportion, and from the subtle modulation of colour, lighting and acoustics. Delight that lifts the spirit and affirms to both students and staff that there is more to education than simply acquiring the skills and knowledge to survive in an increasingly competitive world.

Many people will have been involved in the realisation of the projects, often over many years; in assessing need, in drawing up the brief, in selecting the site, in determining the budget, in securing the funding, in designing the buildings and in the exacting task of construction. The projects submitted for this compendium are a testament and lasting legacy to the efforts of all those who have been involved in their realisation.

With this in mind, the jury was concerned to ensure that no project was judged lightly: all the submissions deserved our full consideration and careful assessment. However, the number of entries meant that it was not possible to include all the projects of merit. Non-inclusion of a scheme should not be seen as failure or rejection but simply an indication that a line had to be drawn at some point in order to limit the number of schemes included. The projects selected are not necessarily outstanding in all respects, but all illustrate an imaginative response to one or more of the areas of interest.

The compendium focuses on the broad areas of interest that are central to the work of PEB: the school of the future; tertiary education – coping with demand; and strategies for managing the educational infrastructure. Each of these major areas of concern embraces a number of sub-themes, all of which have implications for the design of educational buildings.

The school of the future

Developments in educational technology, particularly the increasing availability of personal computers, have radically altered the modes of learning and scale and scope of information available to schools. Many of the school projects include spacious and well-equipped library and information centres. A number of projects demonstrate how these facilities can be planned so that they can be made available out of school hours in order that all members of the community have the opportunity to become active members of the information society. Several projects have recognised the role that schools can play in supporting lifelong education and recreation and have been designed to allow their facilities, such as assembly halls, communal areas and sports halls, to be used by the community.

The growing awareness of the impact of human activities on the supply of resources and the global climate has led to an increasing interest in environmental education. It is encouraging to see how many of the projects make imaginative use of the school grounds to provide stimulating, landscaped environments for outdoor learning. In some cases, the school site has been linked to surrounding parks and playing fields, becoming an extension of the public open space available to the community.

Tertiary education – coping with demand

The recent growth in student numbers and the need for new forms of training related to developments in industry and commerce have resulted both in an expansion in tertiary education and a change in the nature of the accommodation. The increase in individualised learning and the use of information technology to supplement classroom and workshop-based learning in a number of projects illustrate a response to these needs in the provision of advanced and well-equipped new library and resource centres.

Much of the new demand in tertiary education is for courses that are broader than traditional professional and vocational courses. Some of the projects have met this need by providing a greater variety of less specialised teaching space and attractive individual study and social provision that matches the needs of a more socially diverse and younger age group.

A number of projects have responded by providing these new facilities as part of a wider programme of expansion and modernisation of existing colleges. The addition of these new facilities has, in some examples, completely transformed a dull and unattractive building into one that is more appropriate to the twenty-first century and matches the aspirations of the students the institution seeks to attract.

Strategies for managing the educational infrastructure

The design implications of long-term educational change, reduced resources for maintenance, pressures for more intensive space utilisation, alternative funding arrangements and health and safety may not be as apparent in the drawings and photographs used to illustrate the projects as in other priority areas, but they are no less important.

Consideration of the implications of long-term change in education has important implications for the costs of adapting buildings to meet new and unpredictable requirements. Those projects based on framed structures with non-load bearing partitions and generous provision for mechanical, electrical and electronic services will be inherently more flexible and adaptable than more traditional forms of construction. Projects based on pavilion or campus planning will find it easier to cope with any future reduction in demand by adapting surplus accommodation to alternative public or private uses.

Projects with clean simple lines, clad with durable materials are likely to have lower long-term maintenance costs. Similarly, projects with compact plan forms that minimise the surface area of the external envelope will help to reduce heat loss and energy costs. The need to reduce the consumption of fossil fuels and environmental pollution is explicit in some projects, not only in the choice of materials and construction but also in the ingenious use of the building form so as to make maximum use of solar energy, natural lighting and ventilation, and to provide stimulating internal environments.

Greater choice and variety in course options generate a wider range of group sizes. Those projects that provide a wide mix of size and type of teaching spaces, rather than a limited range of standardised classrooms and lecture theatres, are likely to be able to achieve a more intensive and efficient level of space management, as well as providing a more varied and interesting building.

New approaches to financing educational buildings, such as those involving public/private partnership, have not only influenced the plan forms of the projects, but in some instances have made the difference between a new set of buildings being provided or the institution having to continue life in an old and inappropriate existing building. New financial arrangements have shifted the emphasis away from initial capital costs to the overall life costs and have encouraged design solutions that will reduce future maintenance and running costs.

A number of projects involve major additions and remodelling of existing buildings including those of historic and cultural importance. This represents a contribution to recycling and the efficient use of existing resources. Some of them have incorporated new and improved access and circulation routes which, as well as making the building more accessible and easier to use, will also improve safety and security.

One aspect of security which is of increasing concern in some locations is that of theft and the threat of attack or abduction by intruders. The use of the buildings themselves to enclose secure and protected areas, such as the internal courtyards, glass-roofed atria and internal streets included in some projects, can improve security and mitigate against any tendency for schools and colleges to be seen as forts or prisons.

Post-occupancy evaluation

The reaction of the users is an important and often neglected aspect of the appraisal of new buildings. The submissions were not required to include any formal or objective post-occupancy evaluation. However, an opportunity was given for the views of the users to be included. It was encouraging to see how warmly and enthusiastically so many of the users endorsed the projects. They clearly welcomed the contribution that the new buildings had made to the educational and social development of their schools and colleges.

The jury enjoyed the task of selecting the projects included in this second compendium. We have found the variety and originality of the projects interesting and stimulating and have been impressed by the imagination and creativity demonstrated across such a wide range of projects. Only a fraction of the information provided has been included, but we hope that the reader will find something of interest and perhaps inspiration in the projects. With the aim of encouraging the exchange of information and ideas, contact details for the projects have been included. Finally the jury would like to thank those who contributed so generously in providing information on the projects, the staff of the PEB Secretariat and all those who have helped in the preparation of the material for publication.

Michael Hacker, on behalf of the jury
October 2000

The OECD Programme on Educational Building (PEB) promotes the international exchange and analysis of policy, research and experience in matters related to educational facilities and assists participating Members[1] to make the most effective use of the resources devoted to educational facilities at all levels. The Programme has three objectives:

- to improve the quality and suitability of educational buildings and thus contribute to the quality of education;
- to ensure that the best use is made of the substantial sums of money which are spent on planning, building, running and maintaining educational buildings;
- to give early warning of the impact on educational building of trends in education and in society as a whole.

The PEB Secretariat operates within the OECD Directorate for Education, Employment, Labour and Social Affairs. The Programme began as an initiative of European Ministers of Education in 1972, at a time of economic expansion, to focus on the need to provide new buildings for a rapidly growing school population. In the late 1970s, the focus switched to the integration of school and community facilities. This was followed by a rationalisation phase, as governments prepared for a drop in student numbers. Since then the Programme's work has evolved towards its current concerns with the quality, management and renewal of facilities.

The 1997–2001 PEB business plan addresses the provision of facilities for the realisation of lifelong learning for all, reflecting the broader mandate of OECD education programmes. As defined by Donald Johnston, Secretary-General of the Organisation, "Lifelong learning does not mean 'recurrent' training, but a constant relationship with education, starting with an emphasis on 'learning to learn'. And while formal education still represents the cornerstone of teaching, the less formal settings of the home, the workplace, the community and society are integral parts of the learning environment too, just as they are part of the foundations of economies and societies. " *Designs for Learning* presents the activities PEB has carried out in its current mandate, often in collaboration with other organisations specialised in teaching, research and resource management. Each chapter in this book is devoted to one of the four areas of the PEB programme of work:

- improving effectiveness through design and management;
- the school of the future;
- tertiary education – coping with demand;
- strategies for managing the educational infrastructure.

The institutions featured in this publication are listed in the index according to the specific themes within these areas of work that they best demonstrate.

Indicators for evaluating facilities and their utilisation

This book is by nature qualitative and illustrative. PEB, through its work on indicators for evaluating facilities and their utilisation, also seeks to address quantitative aspects and to develop an international comparative database in educational building provision and management.

The OECD has developed a range of indicators in order to provide a comparative picture of investments in education in OECD countries, focusing on educational finance and ownership. The aim is threefold: to enhance individual and collective economic performance through education, to promote the efficiency of educational systems and to identify additional resources to meet increasing demands for education.

Within the Organisation, PEB has undertaken research on strategies for managing the educational infrastructure, on the role of design in improving the effectiveness of schools, as well as on management and the development of indicators for evaluating educational facilities. This places PEB in a strategic position to examine the question of the appraisal of investments in education.

PEB undertook a joint project with the European Investment Bank to identify criteria and methodology for the appraisal of investments in educational infrastructure. The project concluded with the organisation of a conference whose proceedings were published under the title *The Appraisal of Investments in Educational Facilities*. The report aims to present an economic analysis of educational projects. It also focuses on the contribution of performance indicators in the evaluation of educational systems. A third theme concerns the management of physical resources for education, especially the relationship between the school environment and student achievement. Lastly, the report addresses the design and equipment of physical facilities for education.

1 **PEB Members and Associate Members in 2000**: Australia, Austria, Czech Republic, Finland, France, Greece, Iceland, Ireland, Korea, Mexico, Netherlands, New Zealand, Portugal, Spain, Sweden, Switzerland, Turkey, United Kingdom, Albania Education Development Project, Het Gemeenschapsonderwijs (Belgium), Service général de garantie des infrastructures scolaires subventionnées (Belgium), Ministerium der Deutschsprachigen Gemeinschaft (Belgium), Province of Quebec (Canada), Regione Emilia-Romagna (Italy), Regione Toscana (Italy), Slovak Republic, Tokyo Institute of Technology (Japan).

55 Exemplary Educational Facilities

Chapter one

Improving Effectiveness through Design and Management

The schools and colleges featured in this chapter have been selected for special attention because they demonstrate how education can be improved by the buildings in which it is carried out. Evaluation of the impact of facilities on educational outcomes has been a priority for PEB in recent years. Quantification of that impact is extremely difficult, and it has not been attempted in these cases. Nevertheless, it is possible to establish a set of criteria against which to judge the whole. These include firstly their aesthetic appeal, which while partly subjective can also be the subject of common agreement, and secondly, functionality, the appropriateness of the teaching spaces, circulation and other areas to the education programme.

A third criterion concerns the site and the environment of the institution. Some are naturally more favoured than others, but the imaginative use that is made of the site and the integration of the buildings within it can both contribute to education. The quality and quantity of equipment available and the way in which buildings and equipment are utilised to support educational projects are a further factor. The jury also took into account how the buildings are able to provide a comfortable and welcoming environment not only for pupils and students, but also teaching and non-teaching staff, and parents and other visitors. They looked at not only the evidence of the drawings and photographs, but also what the users had to say in written submissions. Where evidence was available, account was taken of the results achieved by the school, as compared with the norm for institutions of the type. Innovation, in design or in construction, was not in itself a criterion, but where innovative approaches had been successfully introduced in ways that supported the educational objectives, this was a plus point.

In the final analysis, however, these nine projects are included here not because they are the best, but because they exemplify, in one way or another, what the jurors felt to be the essential ingredients in a good school or college.

ARCHITECT
Carine Driesmans and Marc Zweber

TYPE OF SCHOOL
Pre-school and primary education

NO. OF STUDENTS
103

AGE RANGE
2 to 12 years

TYPE OF PROJECT
New building

YEAR OF COMPLETION
1997

CLIENT
Administration Communale de Remicourt

At Remicourt the emphasis is on new differentiated teaching methods. The aim is to give each pupil space to develop freely. Based around group work, individual work and workshops, this approach requires a break from the rigid school plan and organisation of the past.

Remicourt's new primary school exemplifies a contemporary design which incorporates flexible, semi-open and multipurpose areas. It provides space for meetings between classes and areas for group activities. The two parts of the building have different functions: one contains the sports hall and cloakrooms, the other classrooms and spaces for related activities. The nucleus of activity in the school is the research centre which includes a library and areas for reading and for individual and group work.

The nursery school is in a large self-contained communal area with a washroom and toilet facilities in the centre. Groups are organised in accordance with each child's preferences and workshops include puppetry, sand play, water play and a do-it-yourself workshop. All furniture and equipment is designed on a child's scale.

A meeting area between the first stage primary class and the nursery class is used by the three primary classes. It also allows teachers to set up joint classes to familiarise the younger children with the work of the primary classes, with the objective of minimising any difficulty of transition to the "big school".

The site for the building was chosen for its central position in the town and the quality of its natural environment, and the grounds are viewed as an integral part of the school. The extensive use of glass in the classrooms and canteen, and the large roof lights, give abundant natural light. This provides a calm and relaxed atmosphere and gives children a feeling of freedom rather than of being constrained.

1

① *Divided into two wings, the school is set in tree-lined grounds in the centre of Remicourt.*

② *The library is set in the centre of the school surrounded by the nursery and three primary class bases.*

③ *View from the entrance hall through a multipurpose hall to the group work area.*

④ *Workshops and specialist teaching facilities are accommodated on the open plan upper floor.*

⑤ *One of the primary class bases, stairs lead up to the upper floor workshop areas.*

⑥ *The gymnasium.*

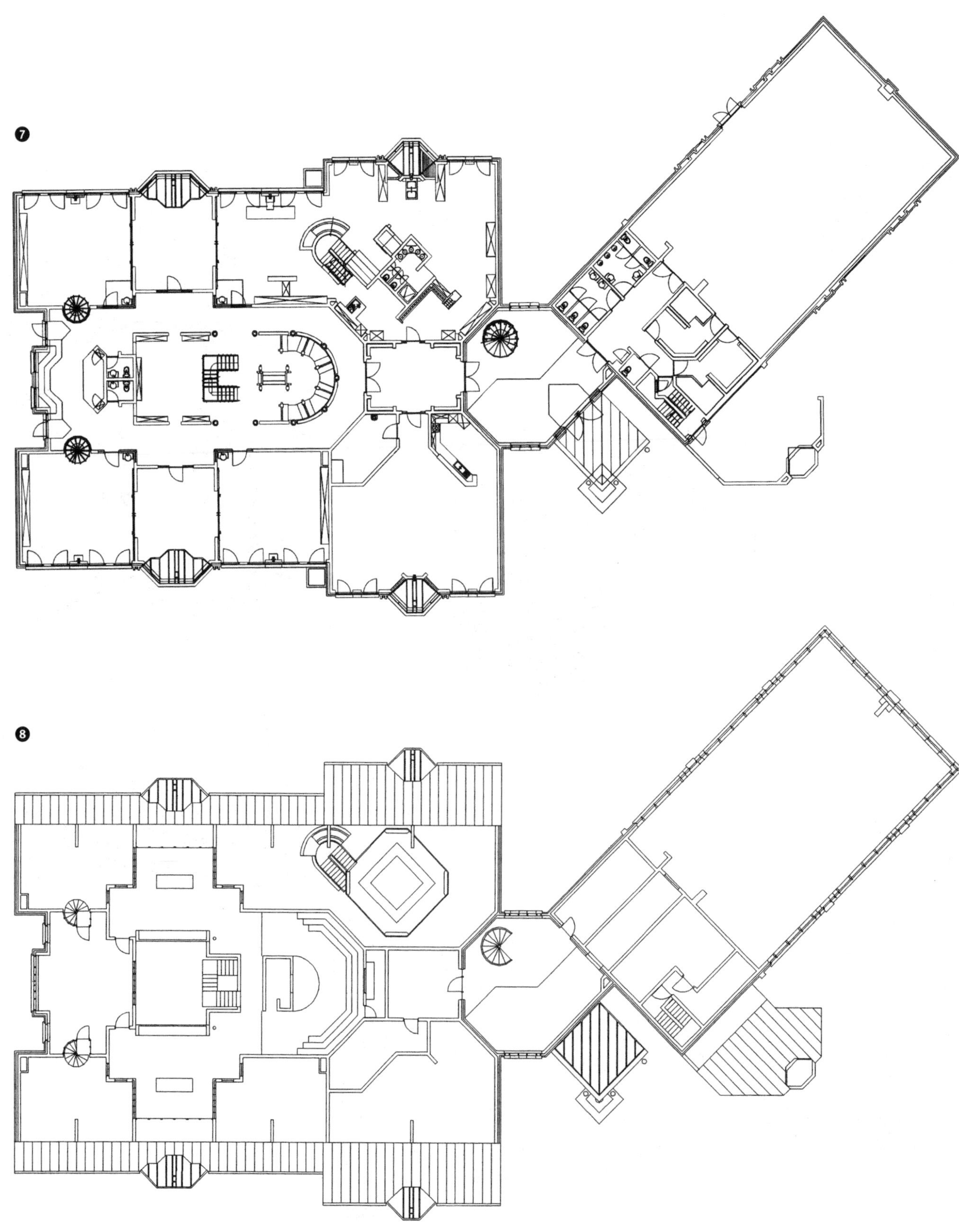

PEB

⑦ Ground floor plan; the class bases in the school wing (left) are separated from the gymnasium block (right). Classes are set around the library and work and play areas. The nursery school is in a large open plan space (top right) in the classroom block.

⑧ First floor plan; workshops housed under the eaves are linked by stairs to each class base.

⑨ The glazed roof in the reception area provides a bright, naturally lit entrance to the school.

"Simple and discreet, the architecture, volumes and materials of this school convey conviviality. The richness of the interior spaces, their variety and functional combinations constitute a new spatial setting, well adapted to differentiated teaching."

ARCHITECT
Ilmari Lahdelma

TYPE OF SCHOOL
Primary education

NO. OF STUDENTS
414

AGE RANGE
7 to 12 years

TYPE OF PROJECT
New building

YEAR OF COMPLETION
1997

CLIENT
City of Helsinki

Catering for a wide diversity of pupils, with children from 20 different nationalities, Soininen Primary School has 12 classes and three special needs groups. Appropriately, the name of this pilot project, which is supported by education departments locally and nationally, means a school for everybody.

Based on the concept of a children's town, the new school complex is designed to encourage pupils to learn through independent investigation and experimentation under the guidance of adults. The different sections are linked by a winding external wall and based around three roofed internal courtyards, or atria, which are also used as recreational areas. There are three main teaching cells – the "suburbs" of the town – which contain the home classrooms.

The separate but related clusters of teaching spaces allow for co-operation between teachers and class groups and, in particular, provide for the special needs of children with learning difficulties while allowing opportunities for integration. Ideas of participation are reinforced by the flexibility of these spaces: partitions and furniture can be moved to allow different classes to be brought together. The hallways of these cells also function as educational areas.

The classrooms, and the three suburbs, are grouped around the school library and information centre. The planning of this shared specialist provision and other common areas – including a theatre, the multipurpose hall and the sports hall – fosters a sense of community in the school and also allows the facilities to be used by the wider community without disrupting the teaching areas. The heart of this children's town, and the main area for social interaction, is the refectory.

The compact plan form, the use of internal courts and the choice of

1

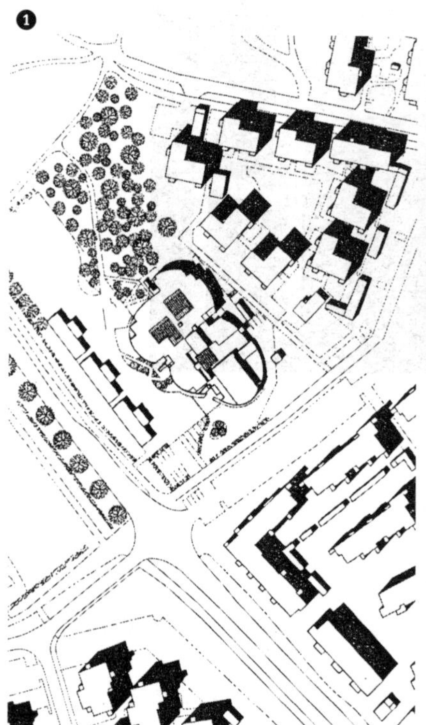

2

materials – brick, wood and steel – are well suited to the climatic conditions and help to minimise energy consumption and maintenance costs. Internal details and well-designed furniture create a comfortable environment at a scale appropriate to the children.

Through careful positioning of the building, it has been possible to preserve the park-like feel of the site and provide spacious outdoor recreational areas. The evenly distributed entrances on the perimeter of the building offer easy access from all directions.

① *The site plan; the school is set in a small area of parkland surrounded by housing estates.*

② *Classrooms are set in two-storey blocks organised around internal courtyards.*

③ *Flowing external walls link the different elements of the school.*

④ *The dining area, the main focal point and social interaction space in the school.*

⑤ *A workstation within the centrally located library and information centre.*

⑥ and ⑦ Teaching areas are set around three courtyards.

⑧ One of the classrooms, furnished and organised to provide a comfortable and appropriately scaled environment for children.

⑨ First floor plan; this floor houses two teaching hubs; teaching areas (A) are integrated with special education facilities (B).

⑩ Ground floor plan; the school is organised around three courtyards (N), the dining area (O) and library (I).

9

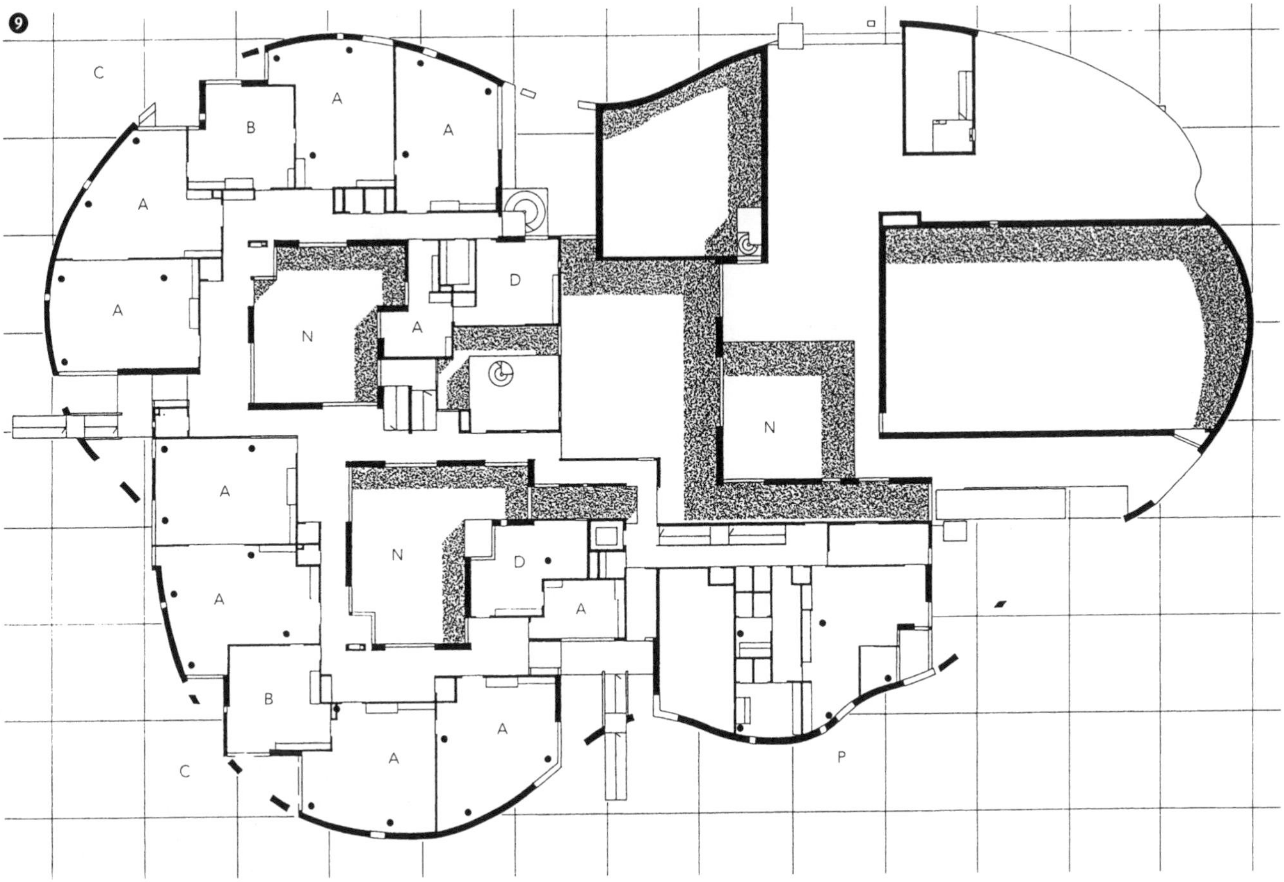

10

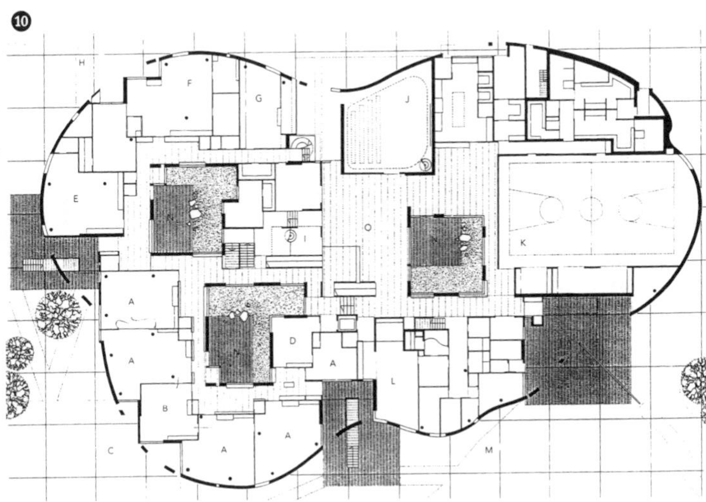

"The detailed design of this small primary school is firmly rooted in the educational objectives of the project. The inclusive nature of the school is expressed in the close relationship of the building to the surrounding park and in the multiple entrances to the building, clearly defined by the flowing lines of the external wall."

ARCHITECT
Allford Hall Monaghan Morris

TYPE OF SCHOOL
Primary education

NO. OF STUDENTS
180

AGE RANGE
4 to 11 years

TYPE OF PROJECT
New building

YEAR OF COMPLETION
1999

CLIENT
Essex County Council

Notley Green Primary School is the result of a competition run jointly by the Design Council and Essex County Council to produce a prototype for a sustainable school – one that is simple to manage, economical, energy efficient and built with the minimum impact on the natural environment. The project demonstrates that a high-quality, environmentally friendly, new school can be built within a standard government budget, and it has helped to establish the principles and methods of construction of a sustainable building.

Occupying a commanding position on the site, the building is oriented so the class bases face south west to maximise passive solar gain and to prevent overheating in summer. This position has been optimised through extensive thermal modelling. In winter, the school is heated using an energy efficient gas-condensing boiler.

With an unusual triangular plan, the school has an excellent wall-to-floor ratio. By reducing the internal circulation areas – there is only one dedicated

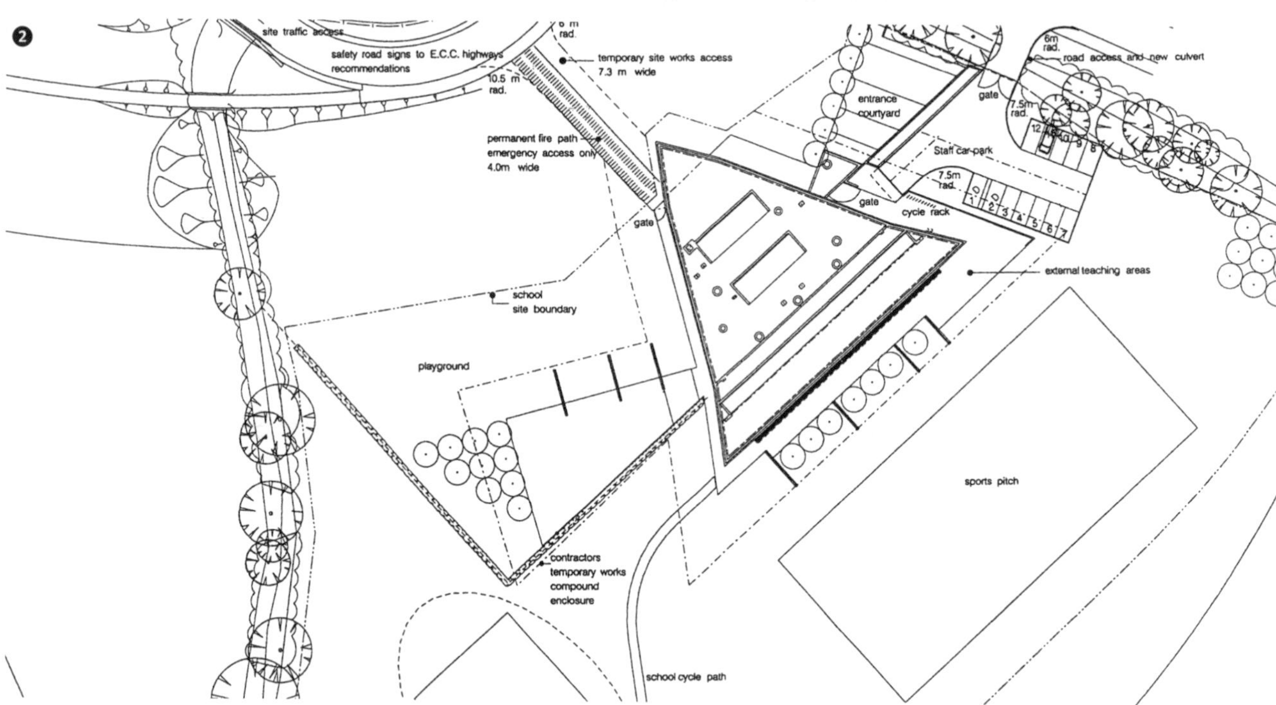

corridor – the architects have created a remarkable amount of space for teaching and learning. The classrooms lead off the corridor, with all other rooms arranged around an internal court. The careful management of space allows more money to be invested per square metre in the fabric of the building.

An external timber-framed "breathing" wall – allowing the passage of moisture out of the building – is insulated with recycled newspaper and is clad externally with untreated cedar boarding. The building has a "green roof" with a sedum mat, filters and drainage membranes.

All materials used have been carefully assessed in terms of quality, lifecyle and maintenance costs, low embodied energy and recyclability. PVC products have been almost completely avoided and recycled materials employed, with worktops made from recycled plastic bottles and entrance matting from lorry tyres.

① *Pupils from Notley Green's first intake in the playground. Designed initially for six classes, the site is large enough to accommodate an extension to the building if required in the future.*

② *The site plan.*

③ *Sliding doors between the school hall and the internal court can be opened out to create a larger space.*

"Notley Green harmoniously combines opposite extremes. Externally, the compact building form and highly disciplined elevational treatment are associated with lively, warm colours. Inside, the enclosed classrooms can be quickly and easily expanded to provide flexible and varied spaces for a wide range of activities, through the use of moveable partitions."

"I like the sedum on the roof so the insects have somewhere to stay and the birds have somewhere to lay their eggs."

Asa Barry Nuttall, age 11

"I really like the idea of having recycled chairs, paper, etc. It saves having to cut down extra trees. I really love the education at this school."

Robert Allen, age 9

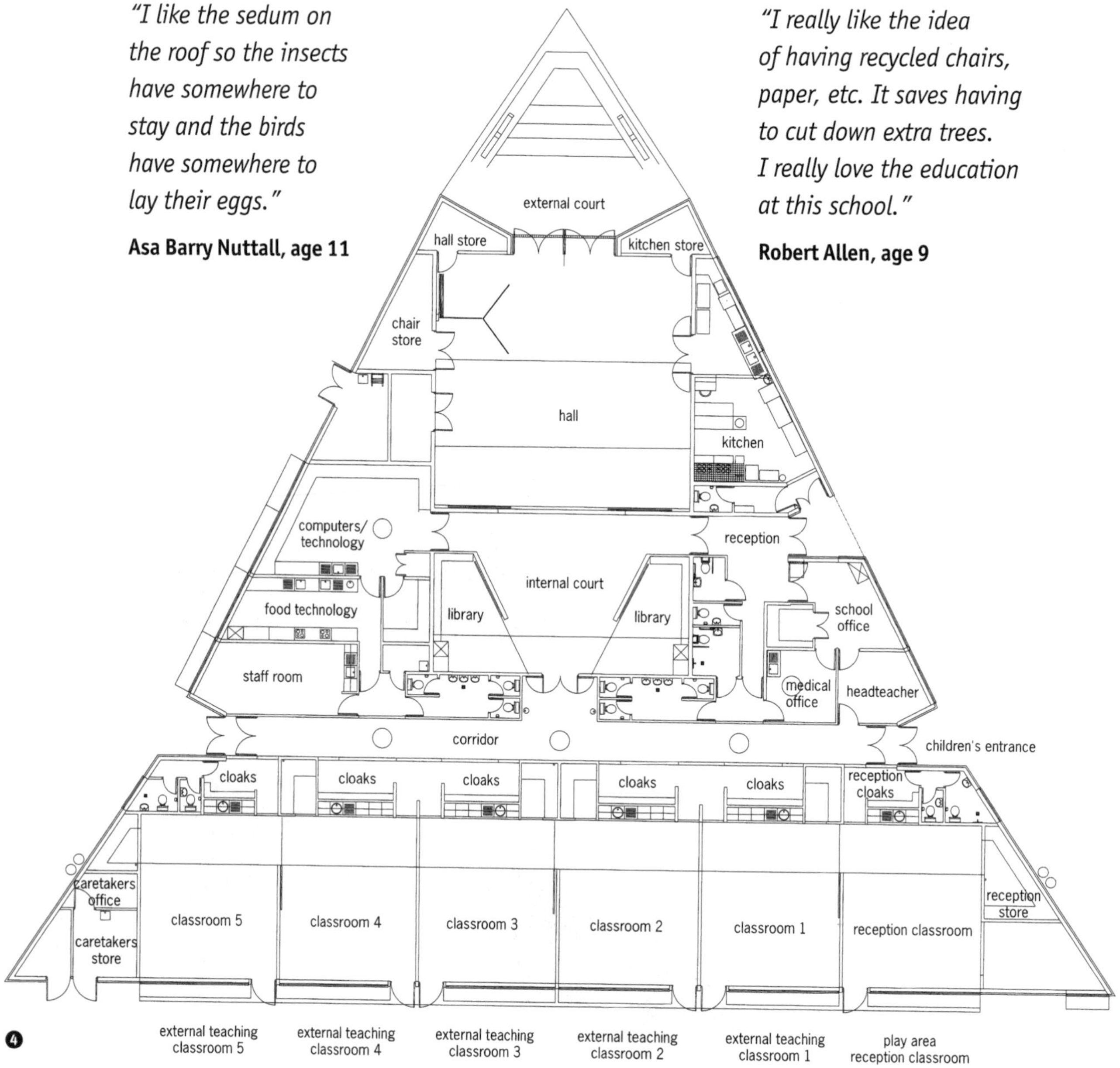

external court
hall store
kitchen store
chair store
hall
kitchen
reception
computers/ technology
food technology
staff room
library
internal court
library
school office
medical office
headteacher
corridor
children's entrance
cloaks
cloaks
cloaks
cloaks
cloaks
reception cloaks
caretakers office
caretakers store
classroom 5
classroom 4
classroom 3
classroom 2
classroom 1
reception classroom
reception store

4

external teaching classroom 5
external teaching classroom 4
external teaching classroom 3
external teaching classroom 2
external teaching classroom 1
play area reception classroom

Natural light and ventilation are provided throughout the school. High levels of daylight are achieved through a combination of external windows and clerestory lights. Roof lights maximise daylight levels at the back of the classrooms and other areas, including the triangular inner court and hall.

5

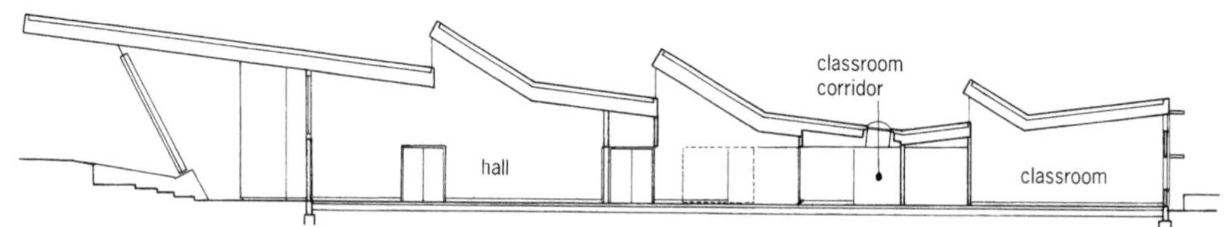

④ *The floor plan; the only dedicated circulation space is a single internal corridor, other rooms are organised around the internal court.*

⑤ *Cross-section of the building.*

⑥ *The "nose" of the building, providing a covered space that can be used for teaching or as an extension of the school hall.*

⑦ *Entrance to one of the classrooms; each classroom has a different-coloured door for easy identification.*

⑧ *The single-storey school is constructed from low-energy sustainable materials; the external cedar-board cladding is chosen for its low maintenance.*

ARCHITECT
Atelier Zo

TYPE OF SCHOOL
Primary education

NO. OF STUDENTS
634

AGE RANGE
6 to 12 years

TYPE OF PROJECT
New building

YEAR OF COMPLETION
1998

CLIENT
Hiroshima City Board of Education

Situated in the hills that surround Hiroshima, Yanominami Elementary School serves the new housing developments that are springing up in the city's suburbs. The school comprises two main buildings which run along the northern side of the large site, with further facilities including the staff room, infirmary, gymnasium, a music room and swimming pool occupying the western boundary.

The external architecture is designed to harmonise with the surroundings. The roof of the three-storey block is styled on a traditional design in this mountainous region. The lower building – which has light brown roof and walls, matching the shade of the local soil – has a slightly curved plan. The overall effect mimics the contours and shape of the surrounding mountains.

The school is designed to encourage respect for, and interest in, the environment. The architect and landscape designer have created a number of different environments allowing children to experience nature from an early age. Attractive gardens are set in the court outside the science and art and craft classrooms. In the playground, there is a stream, landscaped hillocks and a sand play area.

On a second-storey roof garden, there is a small brook, miniature rice fields and small plots in which different types of flowers and grass are grown. These gardens attract many types of insect species including butterflies and dragonflies. Children are able to see dirty water passing through water percolation systems embedded in the building's structure and draining out clean.

1

① *View of the school from the hills surrounding Hiroshima; the school buildings are grouped along two sides of the site, partially enclosing a large play area.*

② *A landscaped garden in the sheltered courtyard between the two teaching blocks.*

③ *One of the 19 classrooms of the school, which serves an expanding suburb of the city.*

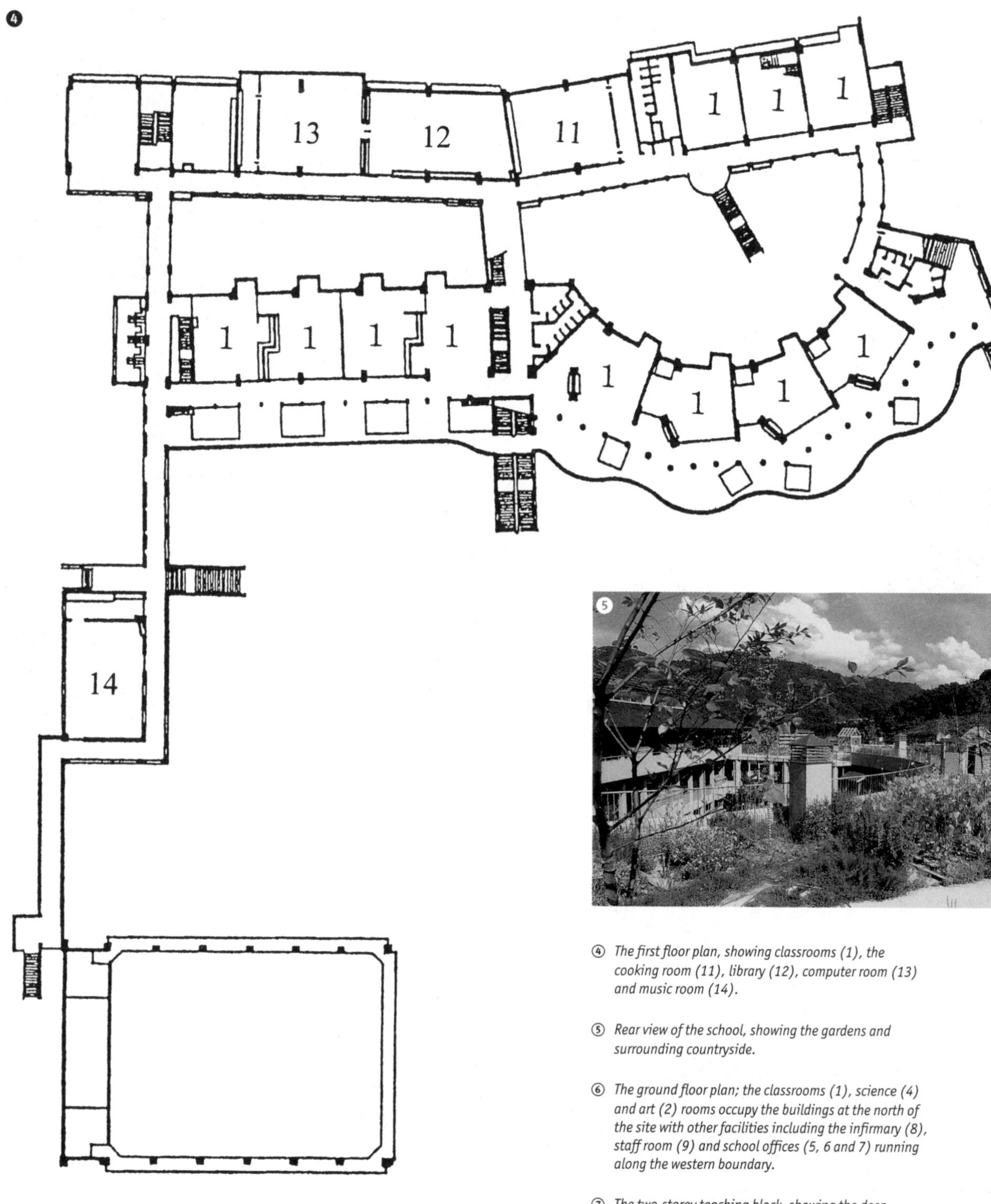

④ *The first floor plan, showing classrooms (1), the cooking room (11), library (12), computer room (13) and music room (14).*

⑤ *Rear view of the school, showing the gardens and surrounding countryside.*

⑥ *The ground floor plan; the classrooms (1), science (4) and art (2) rooms occupy the buildings at the north of the site with other facilities including the infirmary (8), staff room (9) and school offices (5, 6 and 7) running along the western boundary.*

⑦ *The two-storey teaching block, showing the deep sheltered balconies that provide shade, the roof garden and landscaped features.*

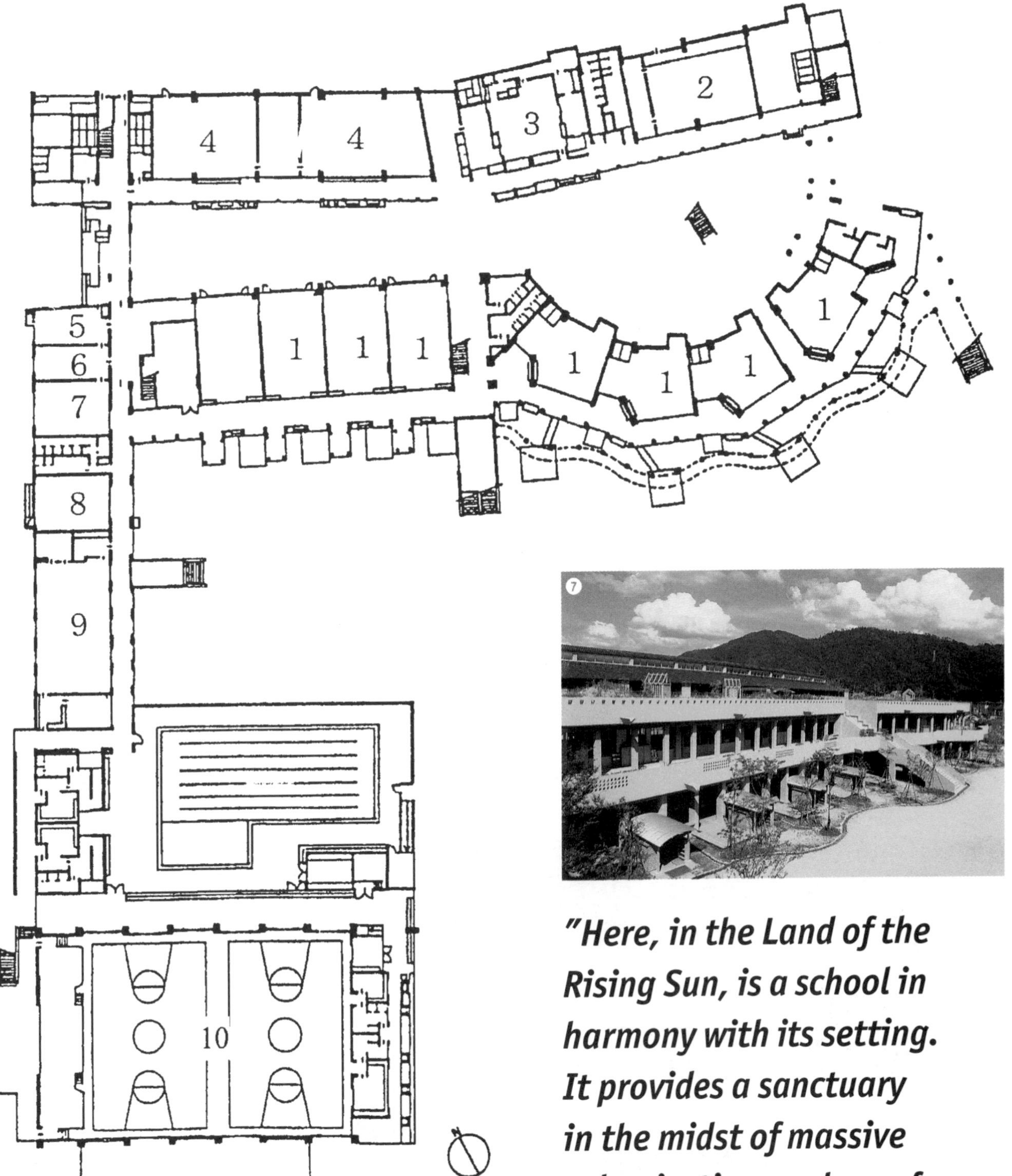

"Here, in the Land of the Rising Sun, is a school in harmony with its setting. It provides a sanctuary in the midst of massive urbanisation: a place of calm and serenity for the 600 students that give it life."

ARCHITECT
NSW Department of Public Works and Services

TYPE OF SCHOOL
Primary, secondary and tertiary education

NO. OF STUDENTS
1 600

AGE RANGE
5 to 18+ years

TYPE OF PROJECT
New building

YEAR OF COMPLETION
1998

CLIENT
NSW Department of Education and Training

Tomaree Education Centre was conceived to replace two existing schools – a primary and a high school – which were struggling to meet increasing local demand for education and were situated on sites unsuitable for expansion. The aim of relocating the two schools to a single site, nearer to their main catchment areas, was to provide modern educational facilities in the most cost effective manner.

This initial idea of moving the two schools to a new site was taken further following discussions with the local council and other government service providers. The outcome is that the centre now serves as a wide-ranging educational and community resource for the Tomaree peninsula. The complex is designed to meet the needs of learners at all levels. It comprises a new primary school, high school, special education unit, health clinic, TAFE (technical and further education) facilities, and a multipurpose centre and sports fields for both school and community use.

The buildings are generally low lying and the facilities are discretely arranged within the campus. However, by bringing together schools and other educational units on a single site, students can benefit from sharing some resources and facilities. There is, for example, shared common space for all ages of learners. The integration of the primary school and TAFE enables joint use of resource facilities such as the library, computer equipment and multipurpose spaces.

The Tomaree complex has built-in cabling throughout, with outlets to all learning facilities to enable flexible access to data, voice and video services. General learning areas have been enlarged to accommodate flexible teaching and learning methods and computer access. A technology unit above the library contains computer facilities and an "open technology" area.

The centre embodies low energy environmental management principles. The buildings are sited and oriented to

1

2

utilise winter sun and summer breezes. Photovoltaic cells generate electricity from solar energy to heat water for the showers and the canteen, and excess electricity is fed back into the mains grid. A ground source heat pump is used to heat and cool the tiered learning space in the primary school. Native plant species are being regenerated on site from collected seeds, and run-off water is collected and used to irrigate the agricultural plot.

① to ④ The individual schools are housed in attractive single- or two-storey buildings, producing small-scale learning environments within a large campus.

⑤ The Tomaree Education Centre (foreground) provides an educational and community resource for the local neighbourhood, bringing primary, secondary and tertiary education together with health care and sports facilities in a single complex.

6

⑥ *Floor plan for the special education unit (block A) and the primary school (blocks B and C). The design allows for the addition of further classrooms (home bases) in the future.*

⑦ *The library areas have been adapted to enable flexible teaching methods and have been cabled for computer usage.*

⑧ *The sports facilites are used by the local community.*

⑨ *The Tomaree Education Centre site plan.*

"Tomaree Education Centre, despite its large size, is an excellent example of a versatile and pleasant small-scale learning environment. The siting of the buildings takes into account the area's natural setting, creating a distinctive and sheltered neighbourhood for every school level and activity."

9

ARCHITECT
André and Christian Roth

TYPE OF SCHOOL
Secondary education

NO. OF STUDENTS
1 500

AGE RANGE
14 to 22 years

TYPE OF PROJECT
New building

YEAR OF COMPLETION
1993

CLIENT
Région Ile-de-France

Catering for a diverse student population, Lycée Léonard de Vinci trains and prepares pupils for 19 different examinations. This new school has been designed to provide a wide breadth of education, to accommodate a variety of teaching methods and to foster a sense of school community and responsibility.

Situated on a relatively confined urban site, the school occupies two buildings, each of which has five levels to maximise available space. The main artery of the school is a large staircase, with its two circular conduits. It links the two buildings, giving access to the canteen, the classrooms and workshops, and the documentation and information centre. Four other staircases help cope with the flow of staff and pupils. Light wells and patio areas ensure that the school is well illuminated by natural daylight.

Each floor accommodates different specific subjects grouped within a broad departmental structure. An office is available to teachers of each discipline. A communication network links each of these offices to the main school offices, to the documentation and information centre, and to the Internet. There are also two dedicated staff rooms located next to five study rooms and two meeting rooms. The documentation and information centre measures 600 square metres and is built on two levels, with

1

small study rooms set aside for individual study or work in small groups. Four assessment rooms are used by students to undertake work under examination conditions.

A responsible and self-reliant approach is encouraged within the school. Students have two cafeterias and games and relaxation rooms set aside for their use. The 230-seat lecture theatre is another focal point for educational and social activities, including staging plays. The 800 square metre school hall, with reproductions of works by Leonardo da Vinci, adds to the school's calm, functional atmosphere. This has helped deliver examination results which are above regional and national averages.

① With a town centre location, the Lycée Léonard de Vinci has a modern and attractive façade.

② Wide, well-lit corridors and stairwells allow easy movement around the school.

③ Spacious social areas, like this area in the entrance hall, provide room for students to mingle outside classes.

④ *One of the classrooms.*

⑤ *The 230-seat main lecture theatre.*

⑥ *The architects chose materials that optimise the use of sunlight throughout the 28 000 m² building.*

⑦ *The two-level documentation and information centre.*

"The Leonardo da Vinci high school is an institution of the future: open to the essential idea of lifelong learning and consequently a place for the wellbeing of the community. In short, an excellent school."

ARCHITECT
Jose Antonio Gil-Fournier Carazo

TYPE OF SCHOOL
Secondary education

NO. OF STUDENTS
1 400

AGE RANGE
12 to 18 years

TYPE OF PROJECT
Renovation

YEAR OF COMPLETION
1998

CLIENT
Ministerio de Educación y Cultura

Instituto de Enseñanza Secundaria "Cardenal López Mendoza" occupies a sixteenth century building, Colegio San Nicolás. Originally founded and financed by Cardenal López, and designed for educational use, the building is of historical importance and enjoys official protection.

The recent extensive renovation programme has sought to preserve the building's internal spaces while enhancing its potential as an educational facility. Much work has been undertaken to ensure that the institute complies with modern building regulations: a lift has been installed to provide access for people with disabilities; a new fire escape has been provided. A more recent outbuilding which housed the toilets has been demolished, and lavatories, with special facilities for the disabled, have been relocated inside the building.

As part of the renovation, the wooden floors have been strengthened and many rooms and original architectural features have been restored. Wherever possible, the building team working on the project have employed procedures and technology similar to those used at the time of the original construction.

The result is an institution where the features of the historic building blend in perfectly with the requirements of modern education. Arranged around the two-storey cloister, which faces the inner garden, are eleven well lit and spacious classrooms where the latest audiovisual technology is employed. On the mezzanine floor there are seven teaching areas where students are offered more personal tuition on an individual or group basis. The restoration has also allowed the institute to transfer the principal's and general administrative offices to a more appropriate location and install dual-purpose classrooms essential for the new optional subjects at upper secondary level.

The restored building is part of an educational complex which includes an outdoor botanical garden, a museum of

natural science with late nineteenth century teaching material, and a gothic chapel which, while still used for religious purposes, is also a venue for cultural events, such as lectures, concerts staff meetings and awards ceremonies.

① *Cross-section showing the imposing main façade of the restored sixteenth century building.*

② *Interior of the gothic chapel, which is used for a variety of institute events as well as for religious worship.*

③ *The renovation programme has improved stairways and installed lifts, ensuring that the institute complies with modern building regulations and improving access for people with disabilities.*

④ *The institute is set in attractive grounds, which include an outdoor botanical garden.*

5

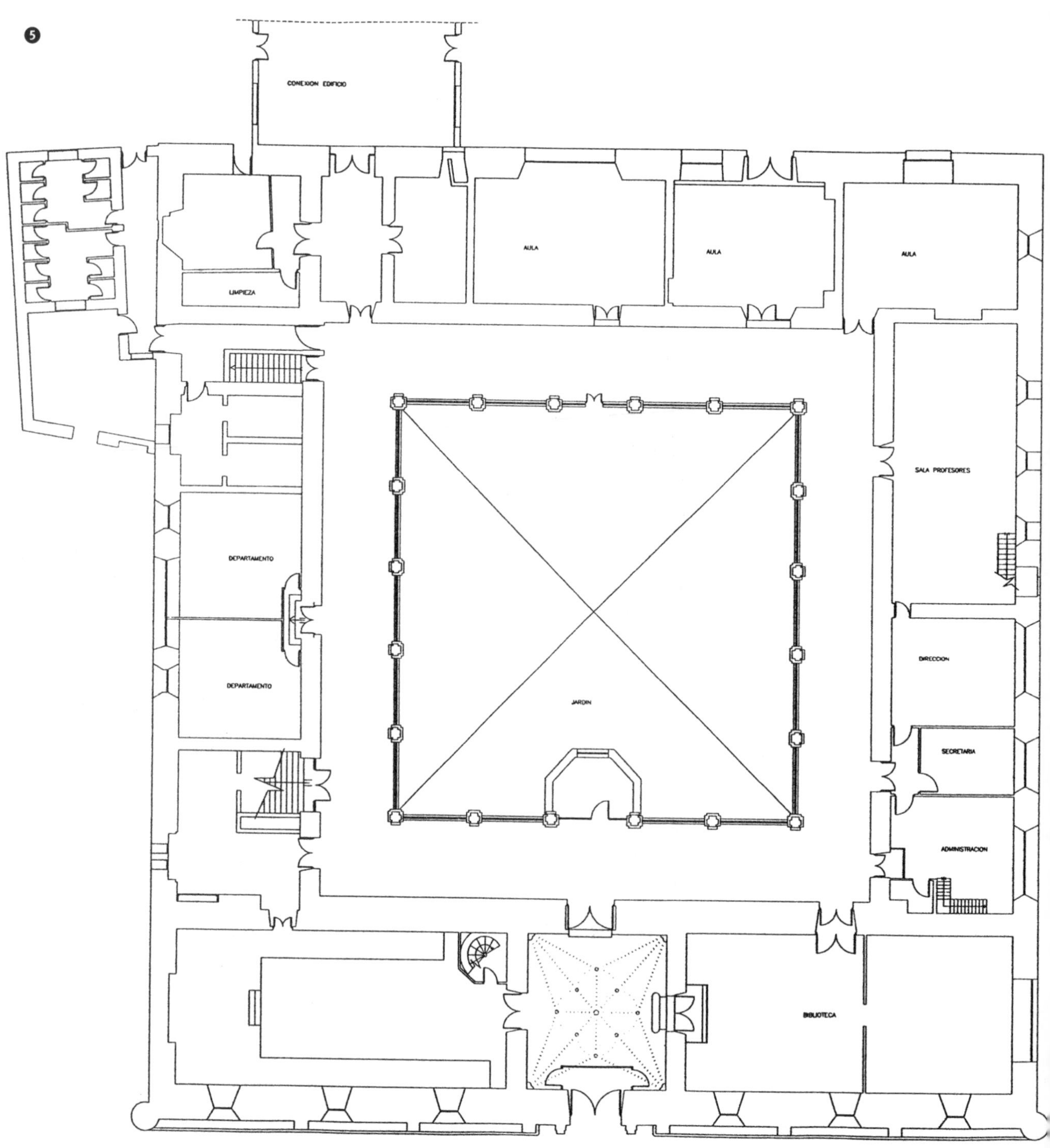
CONEXION EDIFICIO
LIMPIEZA
AULA
AULA
AULA
SALA PROFESORES
DEPARTAMENTO
DEPARTAMENTO
JARDIN
DIRECCION
SECRETARIA
ADMINISTRACION
BIBLIOTECA

"The Mendoza school centre is a successful example of the sensitive restoration and renewal of a building with historic value to provide a modern learning environment that meets today's requirements. The old building, with its symmetrical floor plan, galleries and central courtyard, creates a dignified and inspiring setting for instruction and learning."

⑤ *The ground floor plan; the teaching rooms surround a quiet central courtyard.*

⑥ *A museum of natural science, which includes examples of historical teaching material, is housed within the institute.*

⑦ *Part of the newly restored library.*

ARCHITECT
Rosa Bela Costa and Luis Cunha

TYPE OF SCHOOL
Secondary and tertiary education

NO. OF STUDENTS
1 080

AGE RANGE
15 to 18 years

TYPE OF PROJECT
New building

YEAR OF COMPLETION
1998

CLIENT
Direcção Regional de Educação do Norte

Situated in northern Portugal on a farm where the cultivation of vines and the production of port still takes place, the Rodo school complex contains a secondary school and an institute of professional and vocational education. Other buildings in the complex include student halls of residence, a wine cellar and store, a farm machinery repair shop, greenhouses and sports facilities. The buildings date from different times; the oldest is the original farmhouse, the main building of the old Rodo farm.

The school offers courses in rural tourism and agriculture, focusing on modern technologies and giving increasing attention to environmental protection. It aims to develop in its students an attachment to the region, to help them appreciate the area's agricutural tradition and make them capable of contributing to its cultural heritage. The architecture of the complex contributes to these goals.

The complex was designed to demonstrate a conceptual dialogue between traditional and modern – the new buildings display an architectural vocabulary that is modern but which fits in with the typical buildings of the region.

As well as these aesthetic considerations, the climate, geography and topography of the site have helped determine the design of the complex. The orientation of the buildings, their structural design, the disposition and organisation of their interior and exterior spaces, the shading of the windows and the building materials all take account of the prevailing winds, the path of the sun, and local climate, based on annual sunshine and temperature figures.

Classrooms run from east to west. Buffer and protective spaces, passageways, storage areas and sanitary facilities are located to the north. The south-facing classrooms can thus take advantage of solar energy. To maximise its effectiveness, using a passive technique known as direct gain, the building has a high thermal inertia and external insulation.

The school buildings are designed for environmental comfort, easy upkeep and low maintenance cost. In an addition to using solar energy for heating, air solar panels are installed in the south façade of the school instead of mechanical ventilation systems. These panels renew the air in the classrooms in a natural, controlled fashion as often as required.

❶

① *A cross-section of the complex, the secondary school (left) is joined to the professional school (right) by shared resource and learning areas (centre).*

② *An overview of the complex; the new school buildings (centre) blend harmoniously with the original farm buildings (foreground).*

③ *The complex is set within a working farm, which still cultivates vines and produces port.*

④ *South façade, housing the classrooms and heated and ventilated using passive solar energy.*

⑤ *One of the window panels used throughout the complex; air solar panels above and below the window provide natural ventilation in summer and winter.*

⑥ *The upper floor plan of the main group of buildings in the Rodo complex housing the two schools.*

"The Rodo school centre is a fine example of how to respect local building traditions and delicately combine old and new elements. The potential benefits of solar energy and natural ventilation are fully exploited in many ways in the new building."

6

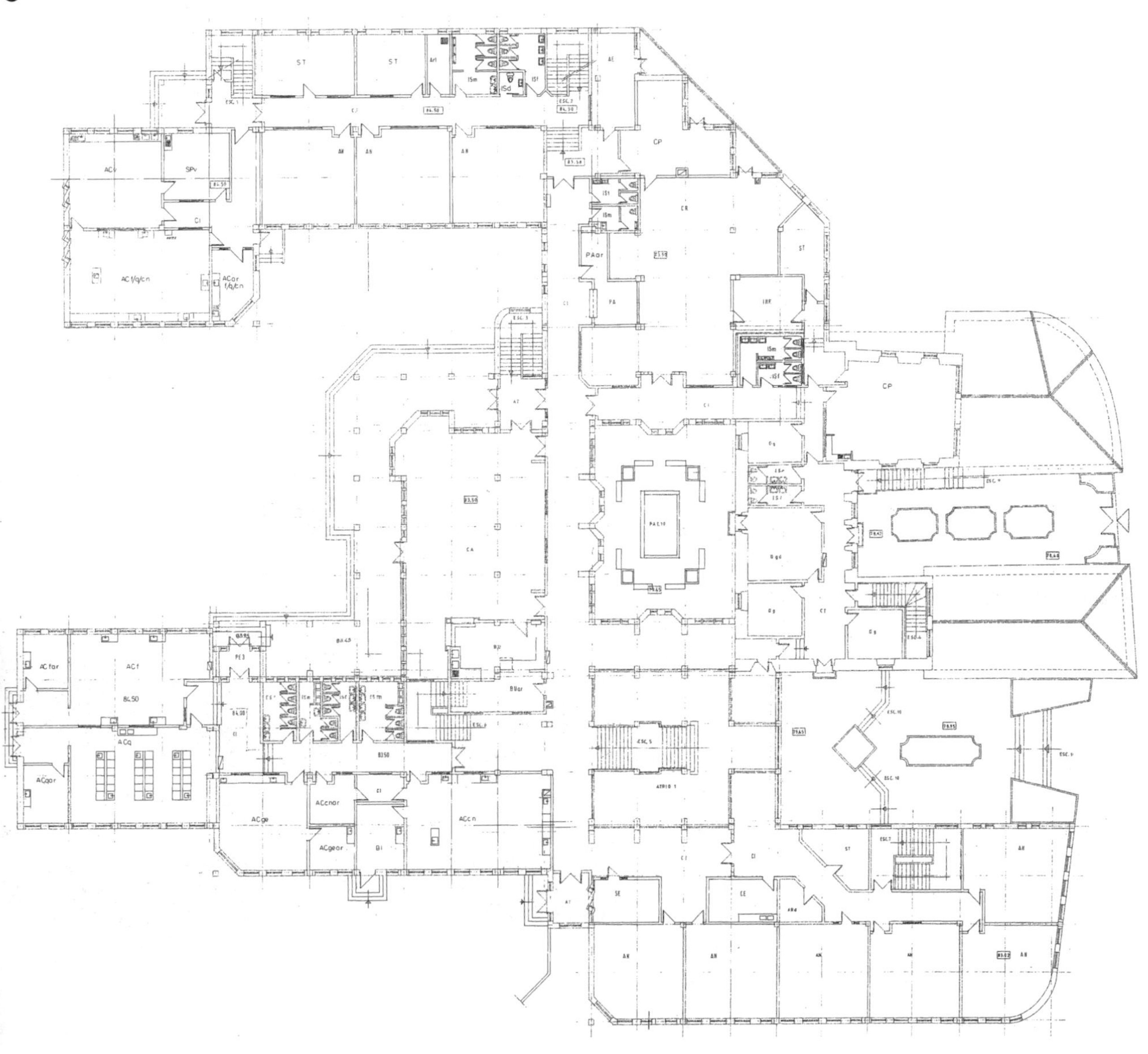

ARCHITECT
Murray O'Laoire Architects

TYPE OF SCHOOL
Tertiary education

NO. OF STUDENTS
2500

AGE RANGE
17 to 25 years

TYPE OF PROJECT
New building and renovation

YEAR OF COMPLETION
1995 to 1999

CLIENT
Limerick Institute of Technology/Department of Education

The master plan for this phased development was based around a large existing single-storey building on a site with restricted access. To provide space for more students and to upgrade the existing facilities, the institute decided to add a new building and completely renovate its existing accommodation, which had to continue functioning while the new development took place.

Now the original building sits on the western side of a new north/south circulation space: a wide, tall, internal street linking the old and new elements on the site. Overhead roof glazing allows sunlight into the street, the core of the new complex; and throughout the redevelopment the aim has been to maximise natural light and ventilation.

With entrances at either end, the new buildings mainly lie on the eastern flank of the street. These comprise a two-storey library over a centralised student computer training area – which has porthole windows to reduce glare and a ventilation system that directs heat from the PCs into the street – and a series of 150- and 100-seater raked lecture halls at ground level. These are custom designed for the latest PC-based audiovisual teaching aids.

On the western side of the street is the administration area. A new three-storey building, it is easily accessible to visitors, students and staff and masks the original building from view.

In addition to providing access to the old building, the library and lecture theatres, there are three points of punctuation along the street, connections to buildings at right angles to the main north/south access: the restaurant and a 350-seater auditorium/conference centre and a multipurpose hall (due for completion in 2001). These buildings complement the more monolithic form of the main spine while creating a pair of external spaces.

The visible and enthusiastic placing of art throughout the building – the School of Art and Design is a department of the institute – is used to enhance and humanise the students' perception of the environment. It helps create a sense of belonging and reduce vandalism. Externally, the traditional brick finish evokes the maturity of academia.

The overall perception of the building, combined with the ability to deliver new courses to diploma and degree standards, has enhanced the institute's reputation. Student intake has increased by 70 per cent over a seven year period.

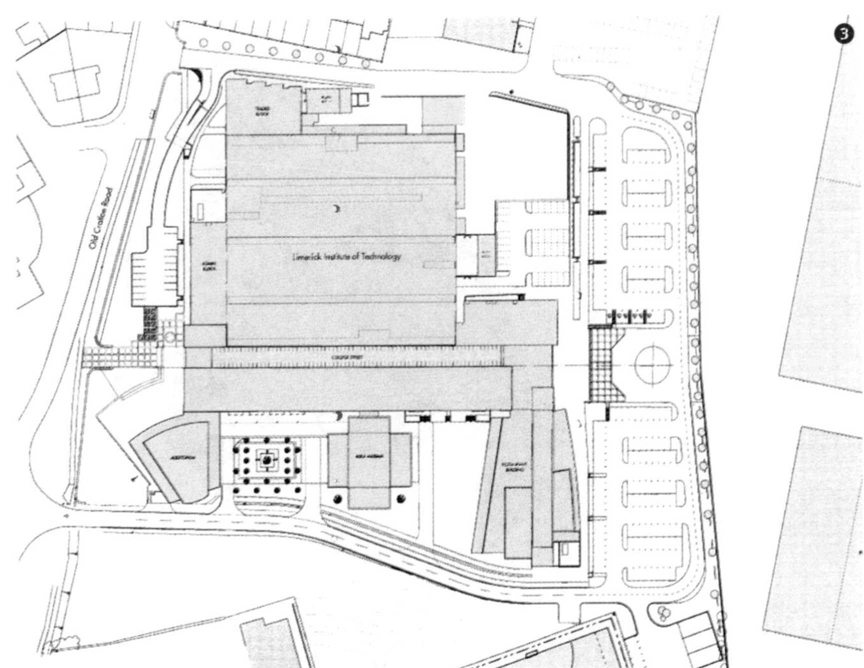

① *Entrances at either end of the college street provide the main access points to the institute.*

② *A view down the street. At this end of the building, new lecture theatres are arranged on both sides of the street; stairs (left) lead to the institute's restaurant.*

③ *The site plan.*

④ *The original building prior to development.*

⑤ *The restaurant building, which is set perpendicular to the main north/south access.*

Photographs courtesy of Eamon O'Mahony

"This imaginative addition has truly transformed the original building and now provides a welcoming and appropriate image to match the aspirations of students in the twenty-first century."

7

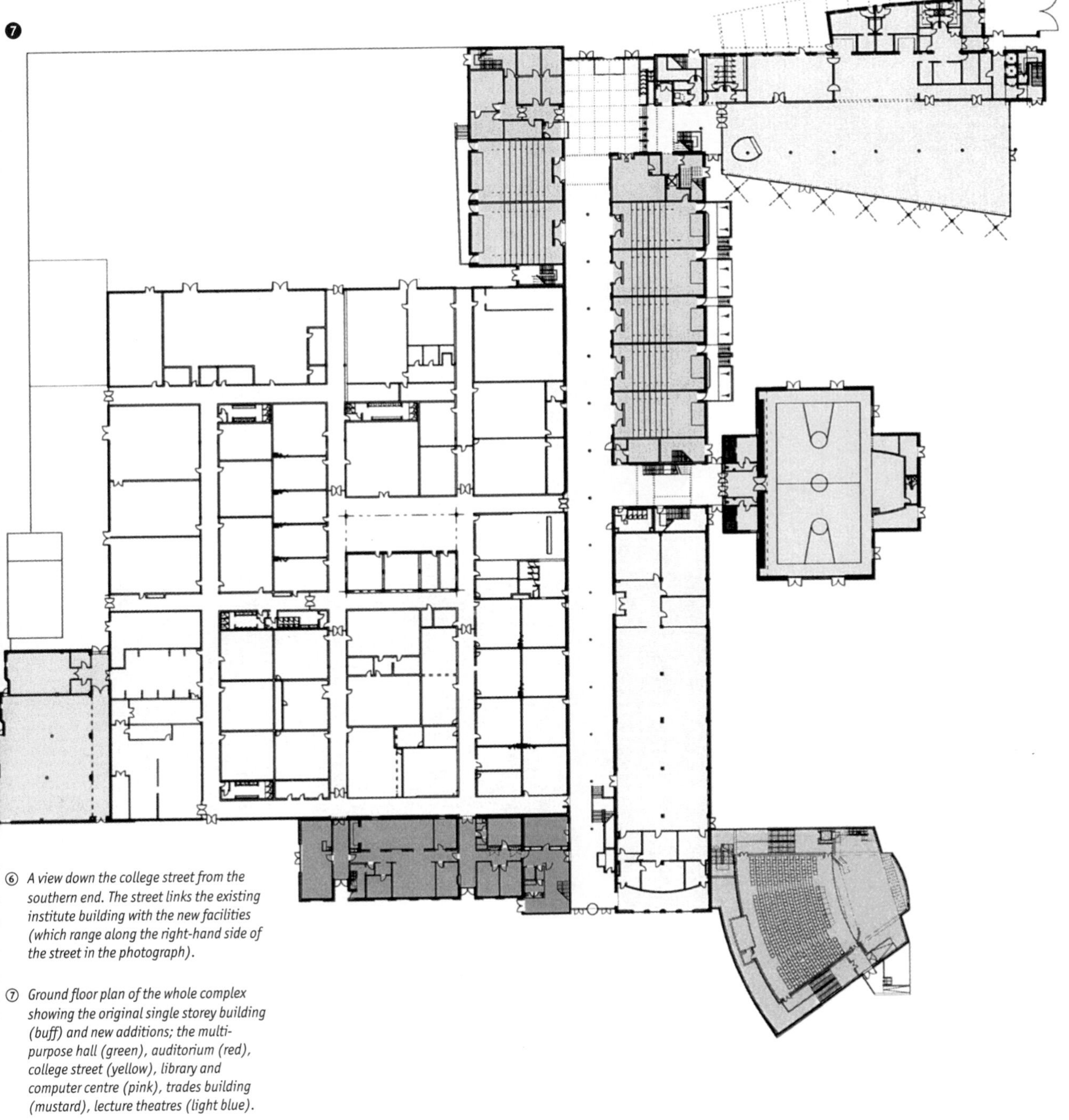

⑥ *A view down the college street from the southern end. The street links the existing institute building with the new facilities (which range along the right-hand side of the street in the photograph).*

⑦ *Ground floor plan of the whole complex showing the original single storey building (buff) and new additions; the multi-purpose hall (green), auditorium (red), college street (yellow), library and computer centre (pink), trades building (mustard), lecture theatres (light blue).*

PEB

Chapter two

The School of the Future

The educational institutions featured in this chapter stand out because of the way in which they respond to emerging trends in learning and society. The unprecedentedly rapid developments of communication and information technology in recent years has given rise to a continuing debate about how education should respond to them and how schools and universities should be conceived. The objective of the work of PEB in this area is to understand the impact on the design and management of educational facilities and to advise on appropriate strategies, with especial regard to the role of the school library and information centre.

Information technology is not the only driver of change in school design. It is now universally accepted in OECD countries that learning must continue throughout life and that adult learning is no longer an optional extra. This places an obligation on governments to ensure that opportunities are provided for all to further their education in formal or informal settings. However, educational facilities are increasingly sophisticated and expensive, and national authorities cannot afford to duplicate them. Hence the efforts of some to group together on one site facilities that are used for adult education, community services and basic education. Several examples show how buildings can be designed to encourage sharing and joint use of facilities.

Thirdly, the schools in this chapter illustrate a growing awareness among designers of the interface between schools and their surroundings, the environmental impact of educational buildings, and the use and potential of school sites. The environment provided by the school, in particular its grounds, is a precious space. In it pupils can experience the wonders of the natural world; they can explore aspects of science, geography and environmental education which need to be learned outside; they can play creatively and enjoy firsthand, often with the local community, the opportunity of developing the school site.

ARCHITECT
Cuningham Group

TYPE OF SCHOOL
Pre-school and primary education

NO. OF STUDENTS
170

AGE RANGE
6 to 12 years

TYPE OF PROJECT
New building

YEAR OF COMPLETION
1999

CLIENT
Kiihtelysvaaran kunta

Situated in a heavily forested area of northern Karelia, the new elementary school at Heinävaara was designed to create a modern learning environment while utilising local materials and labour in the building construction.

Designed to support open learning, the deep, open plan allows a range of interaction between teachers and pupils. A technology and media centre is located in an open area between the classrooms and children are encouraged to work both individually and in teams. Spaces can be easily altered to meet the changing needs of the school.

Local people use the school as a community centre. They have access to the gymnasium and ice hockey rink, and Heinävaara's public library is located in the central area of the school and connected to the media centre. The stage in the area between the lobby and the gym is used by local drama groups.

The school is based on the platform-frame construction system developed in the United States and Canada over the last century. This method constructs buildings storey by storey; each storey acts as the platform for the next floor up. Although it has similarities to traditional Finnish methods, the North American technique is faster and wastes less wood. The school's architects, the Cuningham Group, a firm from Minneapolis USA, sent a team to Finland to teach platform frame techniques to the local building crew.

Drawing on sustainable materials throughout, the basic frame is made from local pine and spruce, with pine used for the exterior walls. With proper painting

① *The floor plan; the teaching and open learning areas (4) surround the media centre and computer area (3).*

② *The main entrance. The wood-frame building was constructed using local materials and expertise.*

③ *A pupil works in one of the study areas. Fixtures, fittings and floors use local pine, spruce and birch.*

④ *The central spine of the school with the media centre and learning resources.*

⑤ *One of the open-plan teaching areas.*

❶

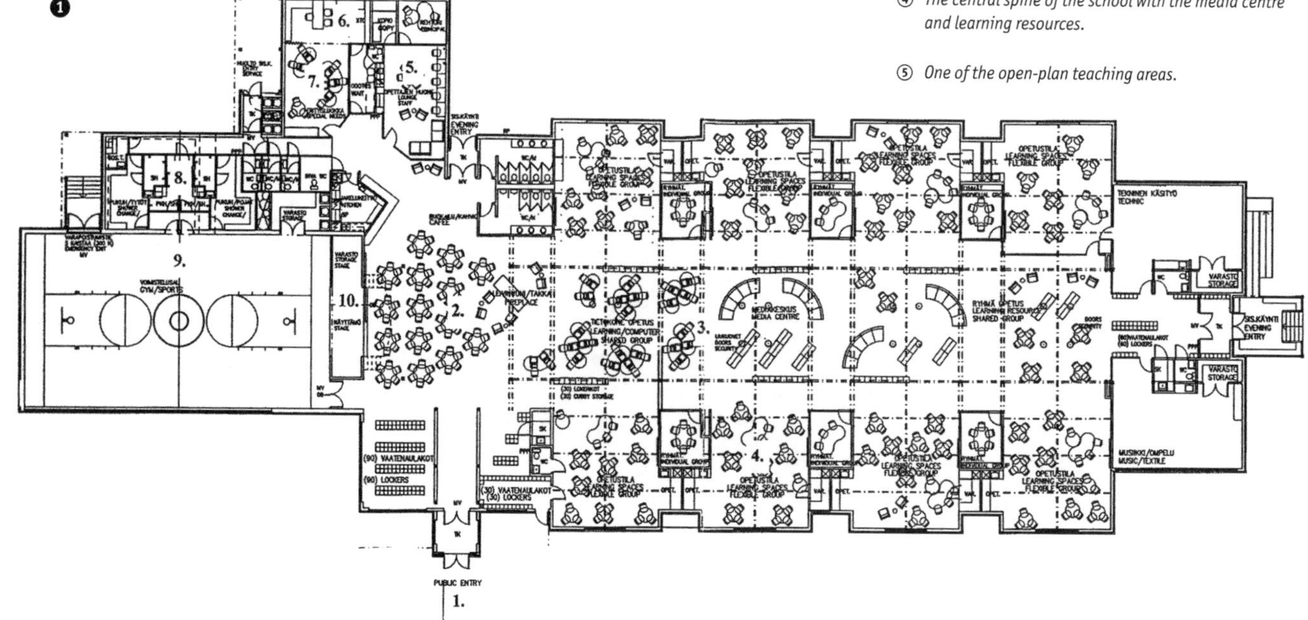

and maintenance, these should last for over two hundred years. Recycled paper is used for insulation; it is installed by a wet-blowing method which makes use of the lignin in the cellulose as an adhesive to keep it rigid. This insulation cuts down condensation, eliminating the need for an additional vapour barrier in the walls.

The heating system uses wood chips delivered by local farmers, and teaching areas are heated by hot water radiators and by preheated air. There is a wood-burning soapstone oven in the dining hall which provides warmth and gives the children an opportunity to learn traditional methods of preparing Karelian food.

ARCHITECT
Alain Chomel

TYPE OF SCHOOL
Pre-school and primary education

NO. OF STUDENTS
350

AGE RANGE
2 to 11 years

TYPE OF PROJECT
New building

YEAR OF COMPLETION
1991

CLIENT
La Mairie de Fontaines Saint Martin

Housing primary and nursery schools within the same premises, the Groupe scolaire Roger Gavage places information technology at the centre of education. In response to requests from children and parents, the school has installed a series of interconnected multimedia workstations which are linked up to the Internet, including two in the nursery school and one in the library and documentation centre.

Classes are encouraged to communicate with each other via email. The use of word processing in written activities is encouraged in primary classes, and educational software is used by primary, intermediate and top nursery classes. These multimedia resources, with their mixture of sound, pictures and animation, have been found to be useful tools for basic learning. Pupils are also taught to search for information on the Internet and use the computer-based problem-solving tools available in the school. Access to multimedia information sources, such as CD-ROM encyclopaedias, is also of benefit to teachers and educational support staff.

The technology does not dominate, and the schools can draw on a number of other resources. The school plan accommodates a range of workshops, activity rooms and play areas. The schools' attractive grounds, which are planted with shrubs and trees and include herb and vegetable gardens, help in promoting environmental awareness.

Teachers of both schools share a staff room, and the pupils' integration is helped by there being several communal areas. The schools share the computer workshop, an audiovisual room and the library and documentation centre – a place for exhibitions, meetings and exchanges between different classes. The nursery and primary classes are situated next to one another, which helps children make the transition from nursery to primary school with ease.

1

2

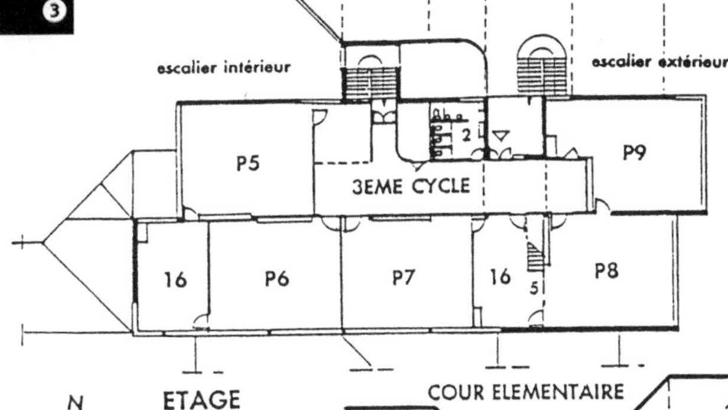

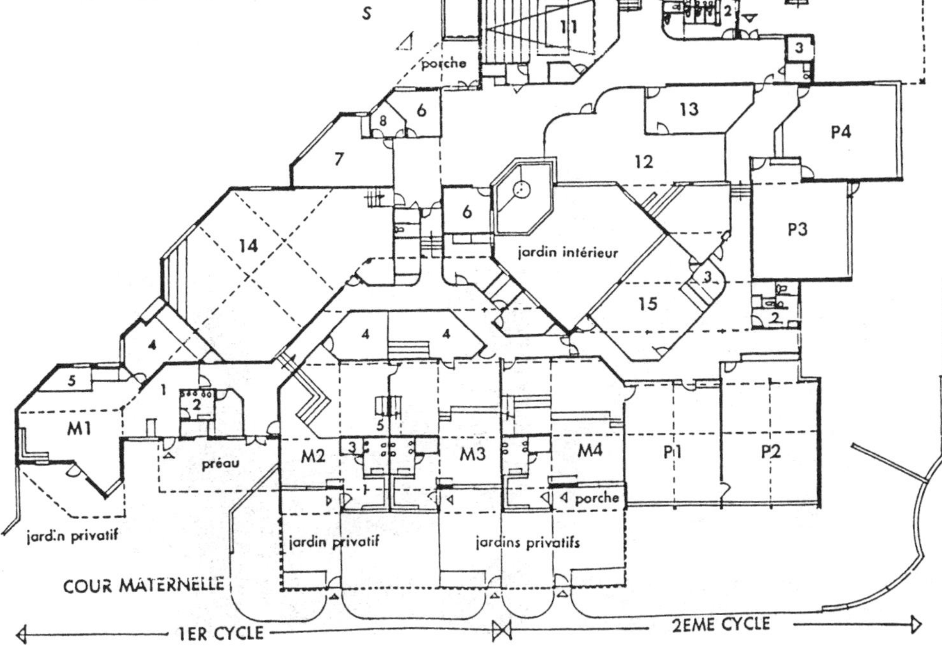

① *At the centre of the complex, the library is a resource for both the nursery and primary schools.*

② *The play room and gymnasium.*

③ *There are linked computers in many of the classrooms as well as in the computer workshop.*

④ *A water feature in the landscaped school grounds.*

⑤ *Floor plans, upper floor (top) and ground floor (bottom); the library (12) and computer workshop (13) are at the heart of the school, the nursery classes (M1–4) occupy the south-west wing.*

⑥ *The nursery is within the main school building, helping ease the transition to primary education.*

ARCHITECT
Architects' office Laiho-Pulkkinen-Raunio

TYPE OF SCHOOL
Primary education

NO. OF STUDENTS
360

AGE RANGE
7 to 12 years

TYPE OF PROJECT
New building and renovation

YEAR OF COMPLETION
1997

CLIENT
Ministry of Education

The Rauma Teacher Training School is a state primary school run by Turku University's department of teacher education. Each year, some 220 student teachers are involved in the school. The facility is also used by the university for educational research, with the focus on integrating pre-school and early education and on the use of information and communication technology for teaching.

Set in parkland, the first practice school was opened in 1898 and then extended in the 1950s. The new school building has been designed to integrate with these existing facilities. It has also been designed to make much greater use of new educational technology.

At the project's inception, teachers and architects discussed how the use of new information technology could change the nature of teaching and learning, and how in turn that would affect the design of the school building. As a result, the new school building provides facilities for pupils to learn independently. In addition to traditional classrooms, spaces for smaller groups and individual work are provided.

The heart of the school is a two-storey multipurpose space surrounded by the classrooms. This space houses a library, several computers, work areas and an expanded circulation area. The classrooms are organised in groups of two, each of which has a shared resource area. All furniture has been designed for flexibility, enabling the formation of different spaces for group work.

Since 1996 there has been an extensive training programme in IT with the result that school staff, student teachers and pupils make extensive use of new equipment and software.

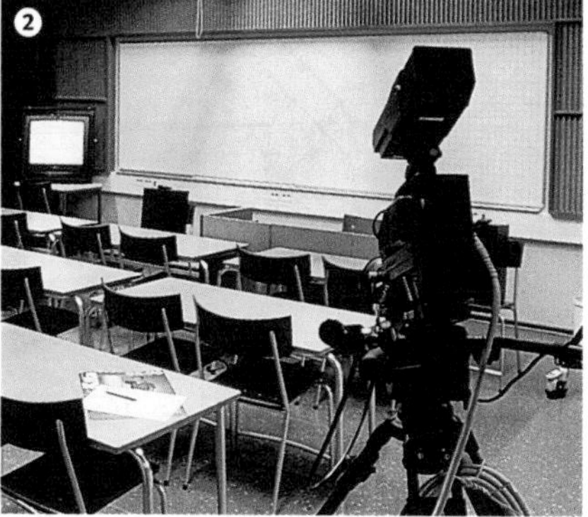

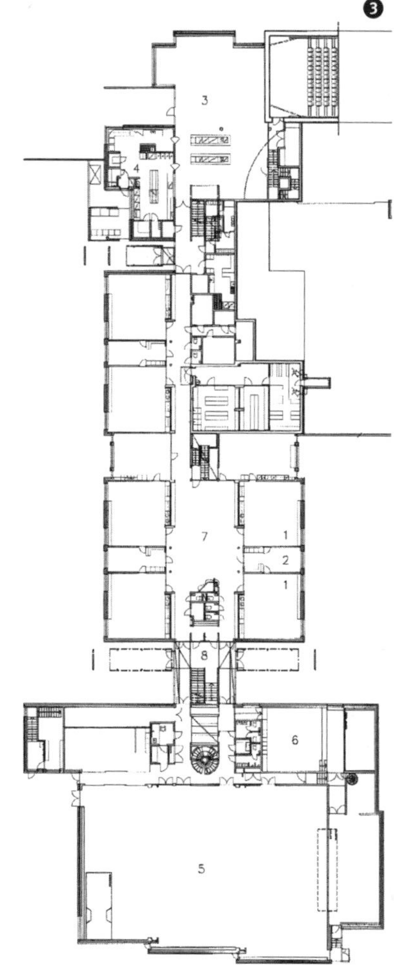

① A multipurpose resource area, at the heart of the new school, provides room for individual and group work.

② All teaching areas have modern equipment to support a range of teaching and learning materials.

③ The ground floor plan: the gymnasium (5) and music room (6) are separated from the classrooms (1) and study areas (7).

④ The school is set in an attractive parkland site.

⑤ The teachers' common room.

⑥ A cross section of the new school building.

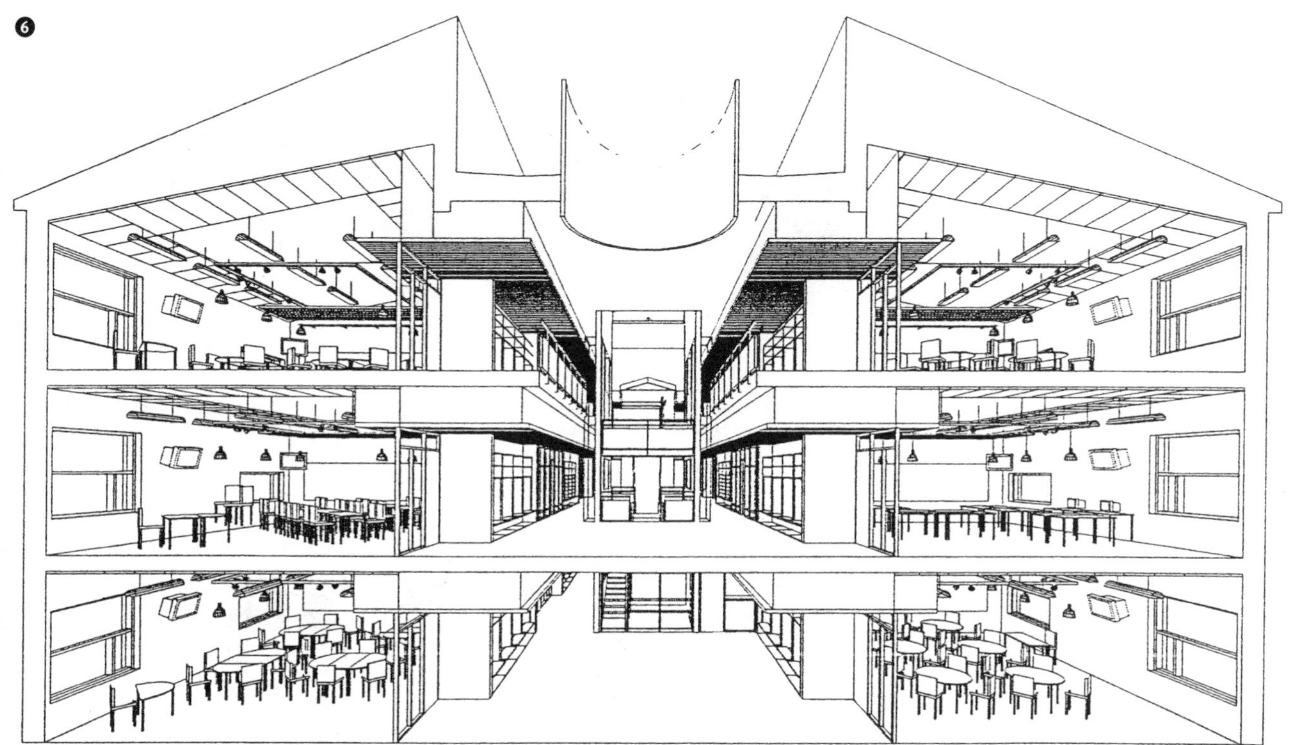

ARCHITECT
João Pancada Correia and Maria Otília Santos

TYPE OF SCHOOL
Pre-school and primary education

NO. OF STUDENTS
576

AGE RANGE
3 to 15 years

TYPE OF PROJECT
New building

YEAR OF COMPLETION
1999

CLIENT
Edifer Construgoes

With a design inspired by the 1998 World Exhibition staged in Lisbon, the Escola Basica de Vasco da Gama is a new building which has sought to replicate the modernity and experimentalism associated with that event. At an aesthetic level, its unusual geometric motifs have been prompted by the nautical theme of Expo 1998. The walls are decorated with wave-like patterns and silhouettes of sea animals, using colours reminiscent of the ocean environment.

The building's design has sought to support educational innovation through the use of up-to-date information and communication technology. The school's IT network has become a key teaching tool, and its resources are being added to progressively and, in time, the network will be linked up to the Internet.

The resource centre contains computer facilities, which will be enhanced through the installation of multimedia equipment. The centre already contains a video and film library, as well as a photographic laboratory. Designed both as an educational resource for the school and a cultural and social resource for local people, the centre can be used by community groups outside school hours

without interfering with any teaching activities.

The school has been carefully planned to accommodate the wide spectrum of ages and teaching levels at the school, as well as supporting an open access policy to the local community. Children of the same age level are taught in coterminous classrooms. The resource centre and management rooms can be reached easily, and communal areas, such as the 200-seat auditorium and the cafeteria, have been situated to encourage both educational and social interaction. All facilities have been designed to require low levels of maintenance.

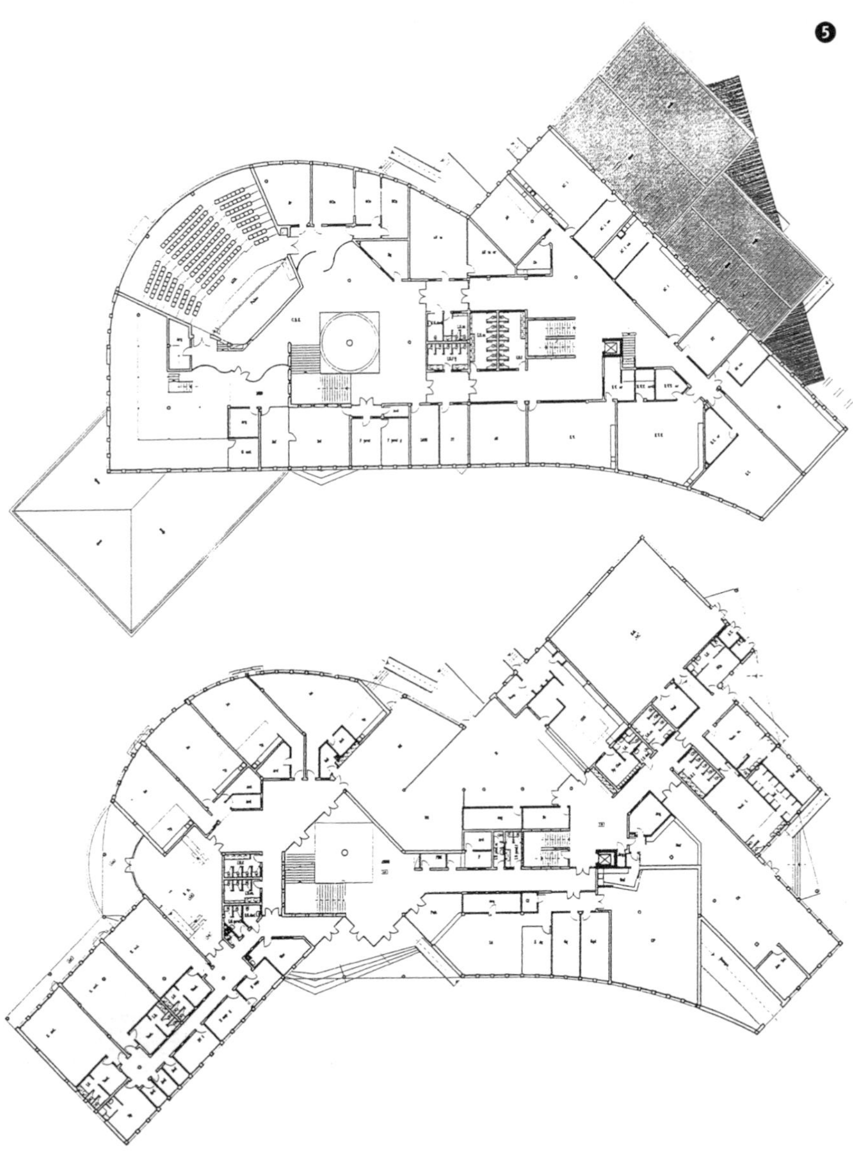

① *The central court and staircase is the fulcrum of the school; the internal decoration has a nautical theme.*

② *The nautical theme is maintained in the flowing exterior façades.*

③ *The rear entrance; the school has an open access policy providing a community resource out of school hours.*

④ *A skylight at the top of the central court brings natural light into the heart of the building.*

⑤ *The first floor (top) and ground floor plans; the unusual non-orthogonal form, with large central circulation spaces, provides opportunities for social interaction and educational activities.*

ARCHITECT
Uti Og Inni, architects

TYPE OF SCHOOL
Primary and secondary education

NO. OF STUDENTS
450

AGE RANGE
6 to 16 years

TYPE OF PROJECT
New building

YEAR OF COMPLETION
1997

CLIENT
City of Reykjavik

The architectural brief for the new Engjaskoli District Primary School was to create a building that recognises the social aspects of being a pupil, with particular emphasis on the space and activities outside the classrooms and teaching facilities – the public spaces of the school. The architects were chosen following an open competition.

The school has a long linear design. It comprises two main buildings: a two-storey block houses the main classrooms, library, teachers' facilities, administrative areas and offices; a lower building contains the workshops, music room and assembly hall. Each building has a distinctive character, with the larger clad with corrugated aluminium – a traditional Icelandic cladding material – and the smaller clad with stucco.

Between these two buildings runs the "street", the main focal point of the school. A light wing-shaped roof connects the buildings and shelters the street. During the day, it reflects natural light down into the street area.

The street is a social space, a place for children of different backgrounds and ages to meet and mix outside the classrooms. To reinforce the theme of school as community, balconies in front of each classroom overlook the street, suggesting the idea of houses and providing a further public space. In practical terms, the street also acts as the main thoroughfare for school "traffic", connecting the main entrances and directing pupils to their destinations.

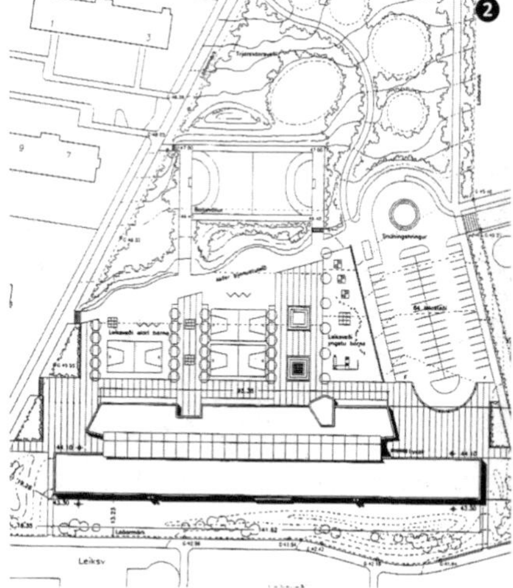
2

1

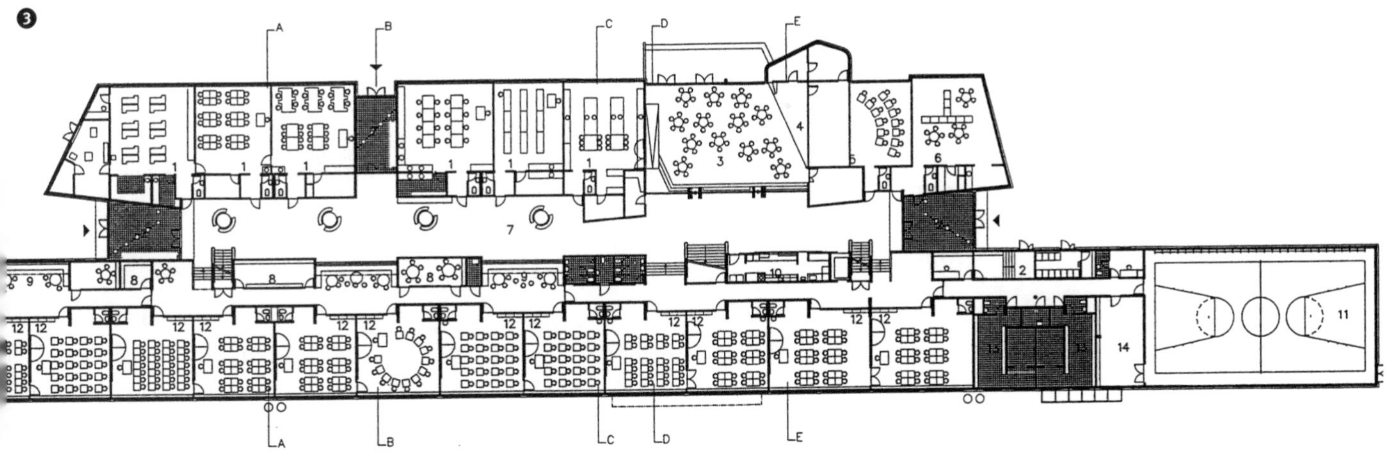

① *Exterior view highlighting the different characters of the two buildings, with the classroom block to the rear.*

② *The site plan.*

③ *As the ground floor plan shows, the school has a linear layout, with the street (7) acting as the main circulation area linking the classrooms (12) and workshops (1).*

④ *The main classroom block, clad in distinctive corrugated aluminium.*

⑤ *One of the school entrances, situated at the end of the street, and showing the wing-shaped connecting roof.*

⑥ *and* ⑦ *Two interior views down the street.*

ARCHITECT
Yapi Merkezi Design Group, Nevzat Sayin and Yildirim Saglikova

TYPE OF SCHOOL
Pre-school, primary and secondary education

NO. OF STUDENTS
888

AGE RANGE
6 to 18 years

TYPE OF PROJECT
Progressive development

YEAR OF COMPLETION
1999

CLIENT
NEKAS A.S. (Company for Qualified Education)

First opened in 1995, Irmak school has recently been extended to allow an intake of pupils up to 18 years of age. The campus now contains a primary school, a secondary school and a kindergarten. The layout of the school and campus reflects its commitment to pupil-centred education.

An auditorium seating 520 people houses a wide range of activities from inter-class events to debates, productions and ceremonies. This auditorium provides a space that can also be used by the local community for conferences and entertainment. A central library contains a variety of learning resources and has Internet facilities – and soon all classrooms will be linked to the network. In addition to the basic classrooms, the school has a range of science and computer laboratories, music, painting and handicraft workshops, and a multimedia centre all housed in the new extension.

All building work has been undertaken in an environmentally sensitive manner. The new extension has been accommodated in the landscaped and tree-lined campus without the need to fell a single tree. The new buildings blend well with the two historic buildings situated on the campus. These have been renovated and one now houses all the school's social, cultural and art facilities. Together they

1

2

comprise a cultural centre which is open to the pupils and to members of the public.

Set in an attractive location overlooking the sea, the school grounds have received particular attention from the architects and planners, and have won environmental awards. In addition to tennis, basketball and volleyball courts and a variety of well-equipped play areas, the campus has an eco-park, hosting a variety of animals and plants. The mature trees on the grounds include a monumental 150-year-old Mediterranean blue cedar. A silhouette of the tree is the school emblem and logo.

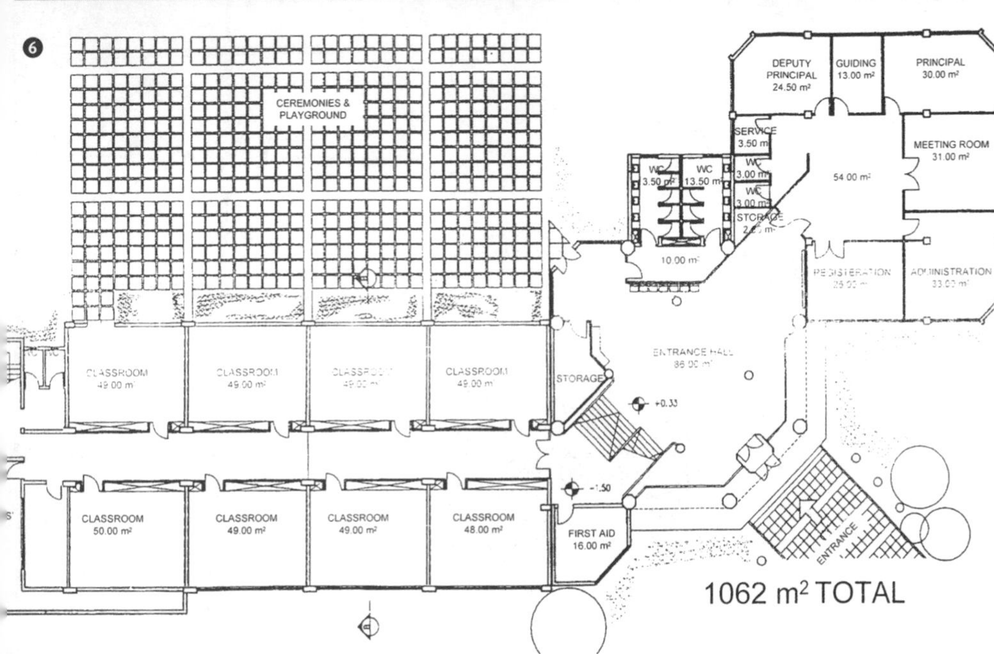

① *The primary classroom block and the media centre.*

② *The new computer laboratories, wired for Internet and individual study.*

③ *Primary pupils making use of Irmak's library.*

④ *The auditorium, which is available for use by the school and the local community.*

⑤ *A view to the secondary school block across the tennis courts.*

⑥ *Floor plan of the primary classrooms.*

ARCHITECT
ARCOTEC

TYPE OF SCHOOL
Secondary education

NO. OF STUDENTS
850

AGE RANGE
11 to 16 years

TYPE OF PROJECT
New building

YEAR OF COMPLETION
1995

CLIENT
Département de la Gironde

A modern school, with stylish exteriors and interiors, the secret to the success of Collège Victor Louis lies beneath the surface. The school is wired up for full multimedia access allowing staff to make extensive use of information and communication technologies.

The school has three interconnected computer science rooms, a multipurpose audiovisual room, and a server which allows multimedia applications to be developed in all teaching rooms. Computer applications with the support of educational software and video material is used in the teaching of all disciplines.

Satellite television stations can be received and there are facilities for putting exercises and lessons online. The school publishes its own newspaper, and new technology is specifically applied to the arts through a computer graphics workshop.

Although new technology is a central part of teaching, the school seeks a balance between technology-based education and more traditional learning and sporting activities. There is a school cultural club which organises trips to cultural and sporting events in nearby Bordeaux. Exchanges are organised with schools across Europe.

In terms of results, rates of progression to year 11 and the number of pupils entering the scientific stream in further education are significantly above the national average.

Collège Victor Louis is a regional centre for learning support, providing training for teachers from schools and educational facilities in the Bordeaux area. It is also open outside normal hours in order to allow pupils with learning difficulties to benefit from its modern technological facilities.

1

2

① and ② *Exteriors have attractive metal and glass details.*

③ and ④ *Colour adds interest to rooms and corridors.*

⑤ *The external features and windows provide protection from the fierce southern European sun.*

ARCHITECT
Jacques Fradin and Jean-Michel Weck

TYPE OF SCHOOL
Secondary education

NO. OF STUDENTS
600

AGE RANGE
11 to 16 years

TYPE OF PROJECT
Renovation

YEAR OF COMPLETION
1999

CLIENT
Département des Bouches du Rhône

The Collège l'Estaque in Marseilles is situated in a priority educational area. Over 60 per cent of pupils come from socially disadvantaged backgrounds. Yet the proportion of students progressing to year 11 are significantly above the national average, and the proportion required to repeat year 11 is below the national average.

This success is largely attributable to the school's use of new information and communication technology. During the comprehensive renovation of the original 1960s building, the school was fully wired up and now every area is linked to the computer network. This means that software can be used in several classrooms simultaneously as it runs via a central server. Similarly, all parts of the school can have simultaneous access to video. The school identifies this as a help in revamping teaching methods, particularly for history, geography, mathematics and science subjects.

There are three computer rooms separate from the main classrooms. In the massive information and documentation centre, students can do their own computer work and make Internet searches. The picture windows in the centre give extensive views over the sea and Marseilles port.

The renovation also sought to improve the school environment. The overall design has tried to ensure that rooms, corridors and walkways receive plenty of natural light, making for free and easy movement about the school. These factors have contributed to a broad behavioural change at the school. Along with its educational successes, there has been a reduction in acts of violence and vandalism and an increase in civic activities.

Importantly, the school has also sought to become more integrated with the local community. Set in a tough city neighbourhood, it has sought to build community links by opening up the 150-seat lecture theatre for exhibitions, concerts and plays, and for presenting the work of the pupils and teachers to parents, relatives and local residents.

1

2

3

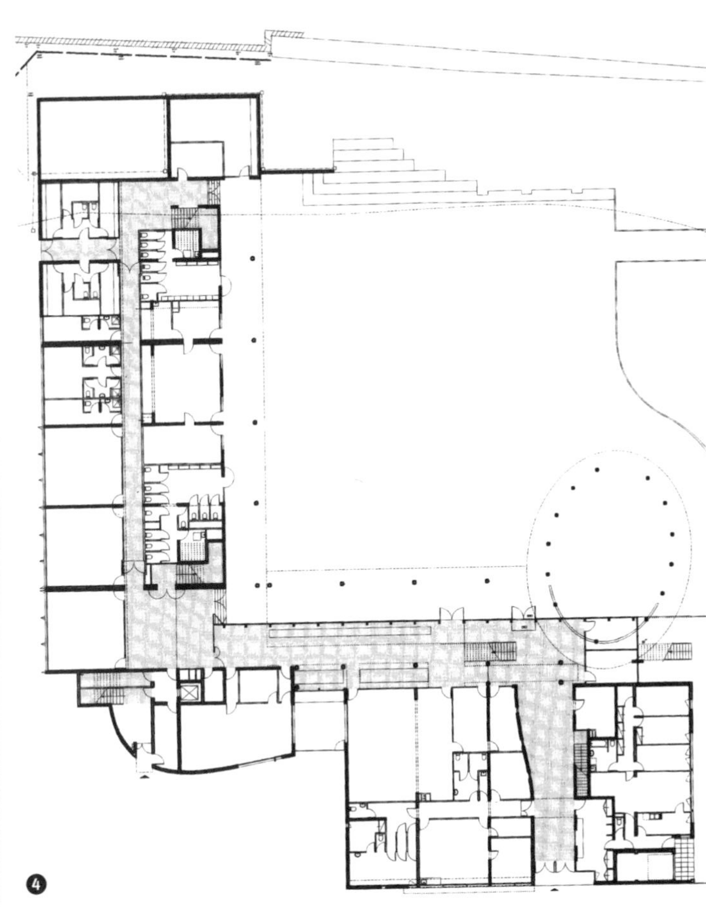

4

5

① *The renovation has sought to harmonise the school with its local environment.*

② *Walkways are bright and naturally lit, contributing to a reduction in violence and vandalism.*

③ *One of the light and airy internal circulation spaces.*

④ *The ground floor site plan.*

⑤ *Exterior, looking towards the larch-panelled lecture theatre and the information and documentation centre, with views across the port of Marseilles.*

ARCHITECT
Gülsün Saglamer and Meltem Aksoy

TYPE OF SCHOOL
Pre-school education

NO. OF STUDENTS
200

AGE RANGE
3 to 6 years

TYPE OF PROJECT
New building

YEAR OF COMPLETION
1999

CLIENT
ITU Development Foundation

Located on the Ayazaga campus, the nursery school accommodates children of the university's administrative and academic staff from three to six years old. Funded from a donation of the alumnus of ITU, Dr. Sedat Üründül, the primary architectural brief was to "design a building that young children can relate to, comprehend and define". Perhaps more fundamentally, the structure also had to be built to withstand earthquakes.

The two-storey building has three curvilinear wings, incorporating group rooms for different age groups, a computer room, a reading room, a music room, a gymnasium and a Montessori class. The outdoor areas are designed for play, for gardening and for keeping pets and allow the children to enjoy the environment and facilities of the campus.

The nursery school is oriented so that its back faces north, giving all group rooms a south-facing aspect and a view of woodland. The form of the building itself defines the area of the southern playground and garden. The north-western wing is allocated mainly to administrative offices and staff rooms.

Reinforced concrete and steel are used for the three main structural elements of the building, while brick is used for the

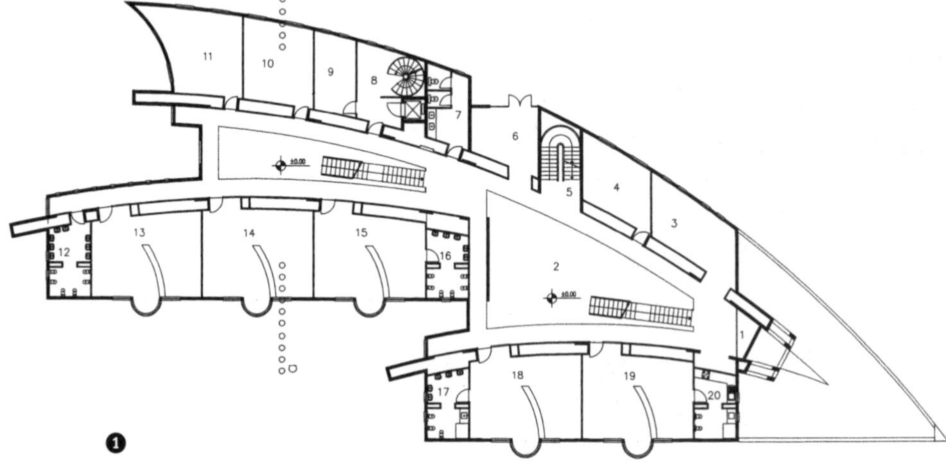

interior walls for durability and ease of maintenance. The atrium area is glazed from ground level to the top of the first floor, which allows plenty of natural light and emphasises its role as a transition zone – visually between floors, between indoors and outdoors, and at the meeting point of the three wings. Although the main function of the ramp in the atrium is to allow safe vertical circulation between floors, it was also designed to be visually stimulating for the children.

The open design allows clear sightlines between and across the three wings of the building. This helps to facilitate the continuous supervision required for pre-school children, while creating an atmosphere that emphasises the sharing of space within the building.

① *Ground floor plan showing entrance hall (1), art rooms (10, 11), group rooms for 0- to 1-year-olds (19), 1- to 2-year-olds (18), 2- to 3-year-olds (15) and 4- to 5-year-olds (13, 14).*

② *Playground.*

③ *Southern façade.*

④ *Computer laboratory.*

⑤ *Multifunctional atrium.*

⑥ *The ramp.*

ARCHITECT
Yves A. Lepère and Frédéric Andrieux

TYPE OF SCHOOL
Pre-school and primary education

NO. OF STUDENTS
140

AGE RANGE
3 to 12 years

TYPE OF PROJECT
New building

YEAR OF COMPLETION
1998

CLIENT
Animation-Education ASBL

Located on the site of a former railway station, L'Autre Ecole retains the spacious style characteristic of the industrial era. The alternating vertical sequence of brick and glass lends a rich texture to its 45 metre façade.

Inspired by Freinet's pedagogical practice, staff at this primary school are keen to foster an atmosphere of open communication in which children learn as much from each other as they do from the teachers. In order to encourage experimentation, participation and a sense of community, the classrooms are arranged around a forum, which serves as a meeting place for children, parents and teachers.

This central space is also the main entrance for the school. From there, the eight classrooms, library, refectory and sports hall can be reached directly via two lateral staircases, avoiding any need for anonymous institutional corridors. Wooden shelving runs the entire length of the school; laden with objects and decorations with which the children identify, they have enabled a large, new space to become rapidly personalised and lived in.

The architects made a deliberate choice to work with natural materials – brick, glass and wood – which require a low level of maintenance. Glazed on two sides, the classrooms are naturally lit and can be easily ventilated. More importantly, however, the materials capture the values which are central to the school's philosophy: openness, naturalness, strength and integrity.

1

2

3

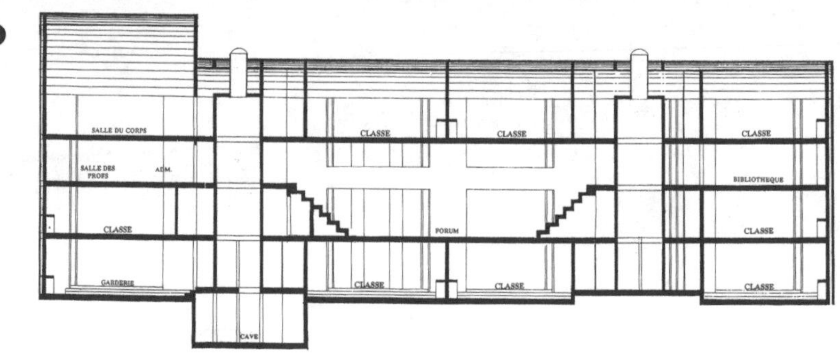

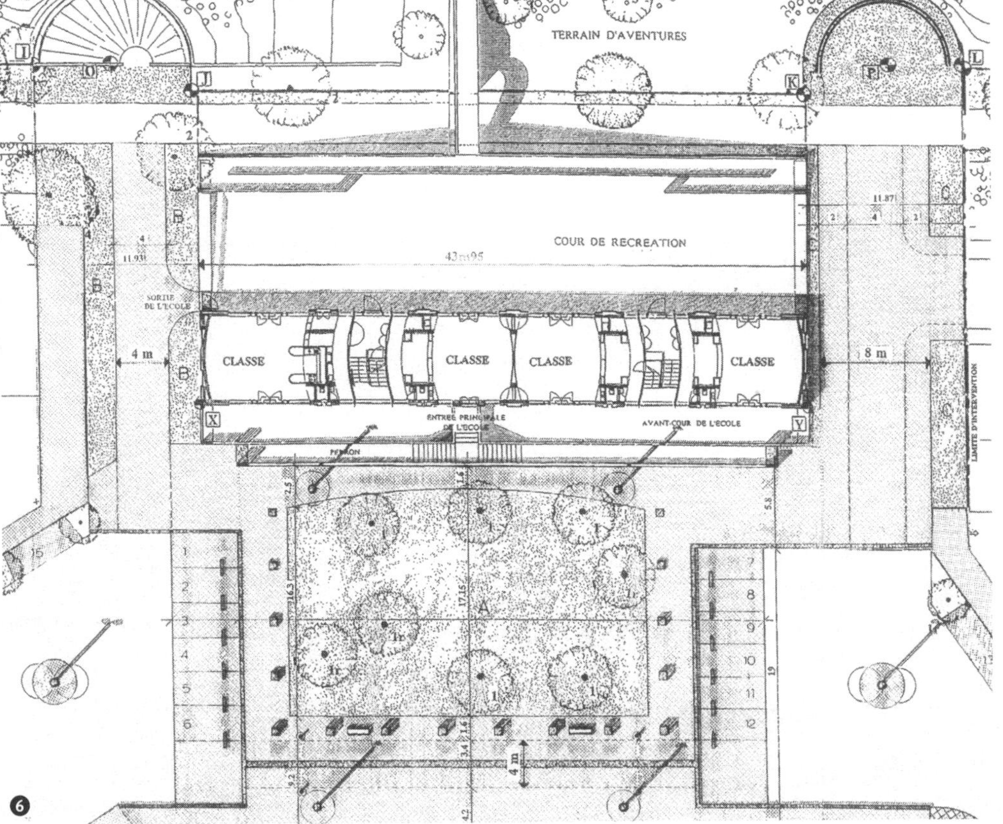

① *The main entrance to the school opens onto the first floor forum.*

② *The alternating vertical lines of brick and glass create a distinctive linear façade.*

③ *The longitudinal cross-section, illustrating the linear format of the school plan (built on the site of a railway station) and the central position of the forum.*

④ *Children are encouraged to place objects on the wooden shelving which runs the length of the main corridor to personalise the space.*

⑤ *Exemplifying the school's approach to teaching, the forum is the focal point of the school, used for meetings and debates.*

⑥ *The site plan.*

ARCHITECT
Stefan K. Hübner with Peter Leibetseder

TYPE OF SCHOOL
Primary education

NO. OF STUDENTS
390

AGE RANGE
6 to 10 years

TYPE OF PROJECT
New building

YEAR OF COMPLETION
1996

CLIENT
Magistrat der Stadt Wien

Located in a new residential area to the north of Vienna, Ganztagsschule Schumpeterweg is a new primary school. The school additionally provides widely-used educational and cultural facilities for the community, serving as a cultural centre along with the local church and the kindergarten.

Aesthetically the building is attractive to adults, yet is built on a scale suitable for children. A backbone of olive-green concrete runs the length of the building, giving it a strong visual identity. The exterior of each of the special function rooms is striking in its individual colour and shape. The school's colourful appearance also distinguishes it from the surrounding residential buildings. Inside, the classrooms make use of natural, indirect sunlight to a high degree.

The classrooms are arranged in a line along a common recreational area. Nevertheless, the boundaries of the individual classrooms and recreational area can be easily rearranged. Individual classrooms can be combined or subdivided in order to create different-sized rooms. This flexibility is further supported by the high mobility of the furniture and technical equipment, giving the opportunity for the school to adopt and deliver a range of teaching styles.

The overall plan combines classrooms, a music hall, various areas for physical education, an agricultural garden, a public library and a multipurpose hall with an integrated kitchen.

The hall can be used as a cinema or theatre as well as a venue for dances and other social events. The inherent flexibility of the facilities makes it easy to organise events such as evening courses, tertiary education lectures and film presentations. In providing for these other activities, the architects have not neglected the school's main users, creating a building with a scale and character to suit young children.

① *The exterior, showing the colourful, joyful architecture.*

② *Library, with amphitheatre-like sitting space.*

③ *Music room, where the seating is arranged in a stair-like manner to give the acoustics the most effective impact.*

④ *The main entrance.*

⑤ *The first floor plan.*

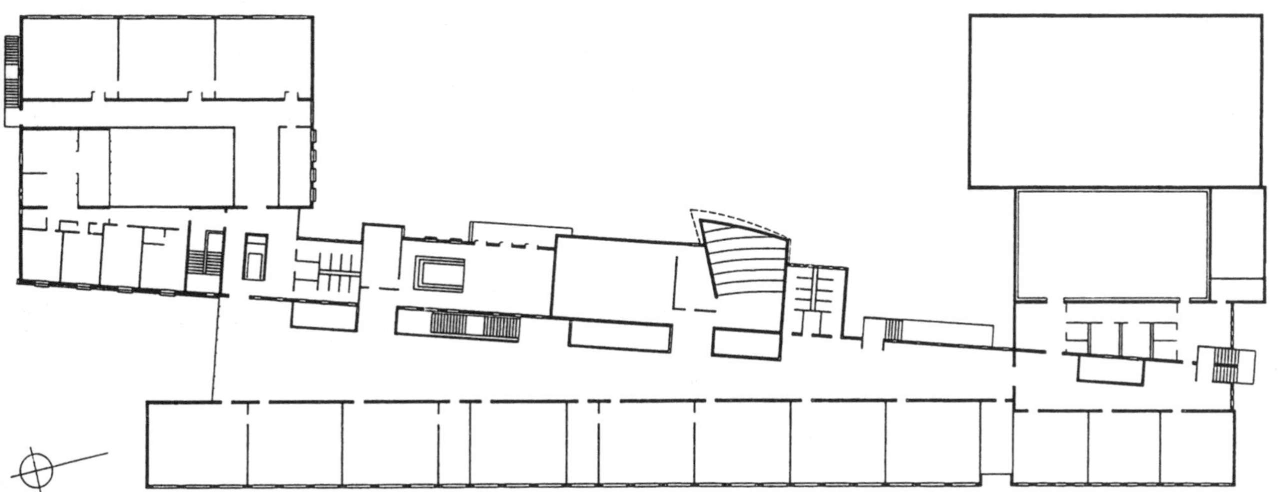

ARCHITECT
José Manuel da Silva Vieira Coelho

TYPE OF SCHOOL
Pre-school and secondary education

NO. OF STUDENTS
900

AGE RANGE
4 months to 6 years, 10 to 15 years

TYPE OF PROJECT
New building and renovation

YEAR OF COMPLETION
1997

CLIENT
Ministério da Educação

Funding for the development of this multipurpose educational facility has been procured from a mixture of local businesses, government departments and the town council. Teachers and parents have helped in improving its facilities, many of which are open to the public.

An important focus of the renovation programme has been to preserve the school's rural heritage. An old farm building has been restored with the help of local civil engineering companies, employees of the school and the parents of pupils. It contains a recreation room, where clubs can hold meetings, a computer science room for pupils and an area for the local photographic club.

The cellar is set aside for a mini-museum where pupils can keep work of special importance to them, an auditorium designed for lectures and recitals, and a special study room. A wine press has also been restored with financial help from the town council, and vines have been planted so that the pupils, who mostly come from the town, can observe the cycle of wine production.

The games room has been built entirely with the help of companies, parents and school employees, and the climbing wall has been financed exclusively by local institutions and businesses. Many sports and recreational facilities in the school are available for used by local clubs.

1

2

3

An old granite house on the site has been converted, with grants from the Ministry of Education, into a nursery. Although principally for children of teachers and employees of the school, it is also open to the community.

The quality of the indoor and outdoor environment of the school is seen as important to fostering the desire to work and study. A number of attractive ceramic pictures and murals decorate the interior and exterior walls, and the gardens have been redesigned and newly landscaped by a team of teachers, the school gardening club, local companies and employees of the school.

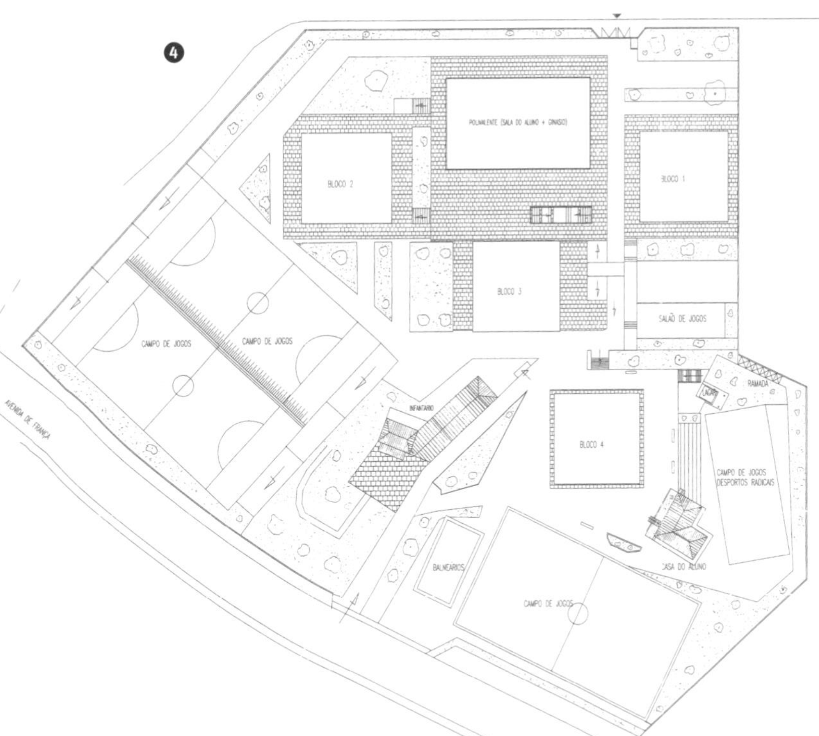

① and ⑥ Attractive ceramics decorate the grounds.

② The crèche and nursery school.

③ Financed by businesses, parents and staff, the games room is a resource for pupils and the local community.

④ The site plan; the site accommodates a crèche, nursery school, lower secondary school and sports facilities.

⑤ The playground, with one of the restored buildings in the background.

⑦ Teachers, pupils and local companies have all contributed to improving the school grounds through planting and landscaping.

ARCHITECT
Fabrica Artis Architects

TYPE OF SCHOOL
Primary, lower secondary and adult education

NO. OF STUDENTS
98

AGE RANGE
6 to 15 years

TYPE OF PROJECT
New building

YEAR OF COMPLETION
1998

CLIENT
Toga Village Board of Education

Toga is a small, remote village of some 1 000 inhabitants situated in the mountains of central Japan. The area is famous for its steep-roofed, old houses, indeed a nearby village is a World Cultural Heritage site. This traditional architectural style has been deliberately reflected in the main roof of this multipurpose facility, a symbolic choice as the building is designed to act as a focal point for the community, providing primary and lower secondary education and a centre for lifelong learning.

This school is built in two wings, one for the primary school – which contains a range of open plan and semi-enclosed spaces – the other for the secondary school. The main shared rooms and community facilities, including the library, are located where these wings meet. These include the more specialised classrooms for teaching cookery, music, and art and craft. The overall space allocation, at just under 10 000 m^2, is generous because several spaces are shared effectively.

Many facilities are shared. Children from the two schools share the lunch room, and both use the gymnasium and special classrooms. Teachers of both schools use a single teachers' room, which allows them to share information on teaching methods and the pupils. Although resources like the library are shared by both the schools and the community centre, there is generally clear separation of community and school facilities.

The grounds contain sports facilities for school and community use. There are also several open terraces sheltered by the overhanging roof.

❶

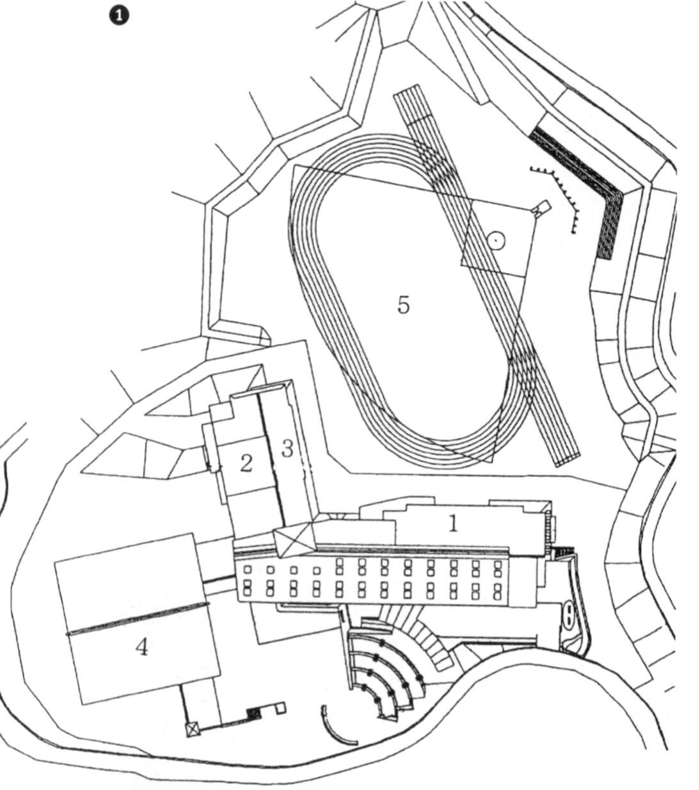

❷

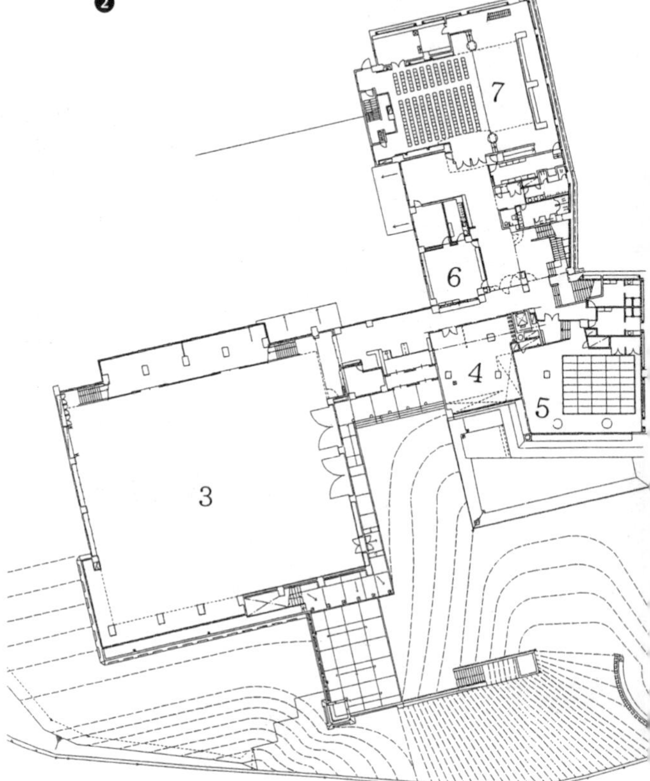

③

④

⑤

① *The site plan showing the primary school (1), lower secondary school (2), community centre (3), gymnasium (4) and sports field (5).*

② *First floor plan.*

③ *The school building has a characteristic steep sloping roof, typical of this part of Japan which has heavy snowfall in winter.*

④ *Secondary school pupils taking an English class.*

⑤ *One of the open plan primary classrooms.*

⑥ *Children in the primary school play room.*

⑦ *The school has an attractive and varied plan, with many open and semi-enclosed spaces.*

⑥

⑦

ARCHITECT
Jack Pattisson

TYPE OF SCHOOL
Upper secondary education, vocational education and training, adult education

NO. OF STUDENTS
550

AGE RANGE
16 to 20+ years

TYPE OF PROJECT
New building/extension

YEAR OF COMPLETION
1999

CLIENT
Municipality of Vaggeryd

Fenix Kunskapscentrum is an upper secondary school and also hosts adult education including SFI classes (Swedish For Immigrants) and university studies. It is the only upper secondary school in Sweden to be built specifically to deliver problem-based teaching and learning. This demands the active participation of students, working together with their teachers – known as mentors in the school – to learn through activities and to seek knowledge from a variety of sources of information.

The school is constructed to maximise the space for independent study. There are no standard rows of classrooms and the teaching facilities and other special areas link to a street that winds around the main library. There are two auditoria, one seating 60 people and a larger one which seats 120. Structurally it is built using a column and beam system allowing the configuration of rooms in the building to be changed for different purposes.

The construction of the Fenix Kunskapscentrum is based around information technology – it is possible for every student to have access to a computer at any time for assignments and research as well as to make use of more advanced equipment such as digital film editing facilities. Sources of information are gathered around subject areas and the centrally located library.

The focal point of the school, the library, contains work sites, learning cells, computers and books. The mathematics, natural science and technology departments form another sub-centre, together with the technical and industrial laboratories. Areas for the study of arts subjects are used for teaching, displaying work and common activities.

The aim has been to create an environment that inspires students in their work and in which communication and participation are seen as vital to the learning process.

1

① *Aerial view; the teaching and subject areas fan out from the central library.*

② *Looking across the main library and learning resource area; students are encouraged to manage and direct their own learning.*

③ *A light, airy circulation space winds round the library.*

④ *The ground floor plan.*

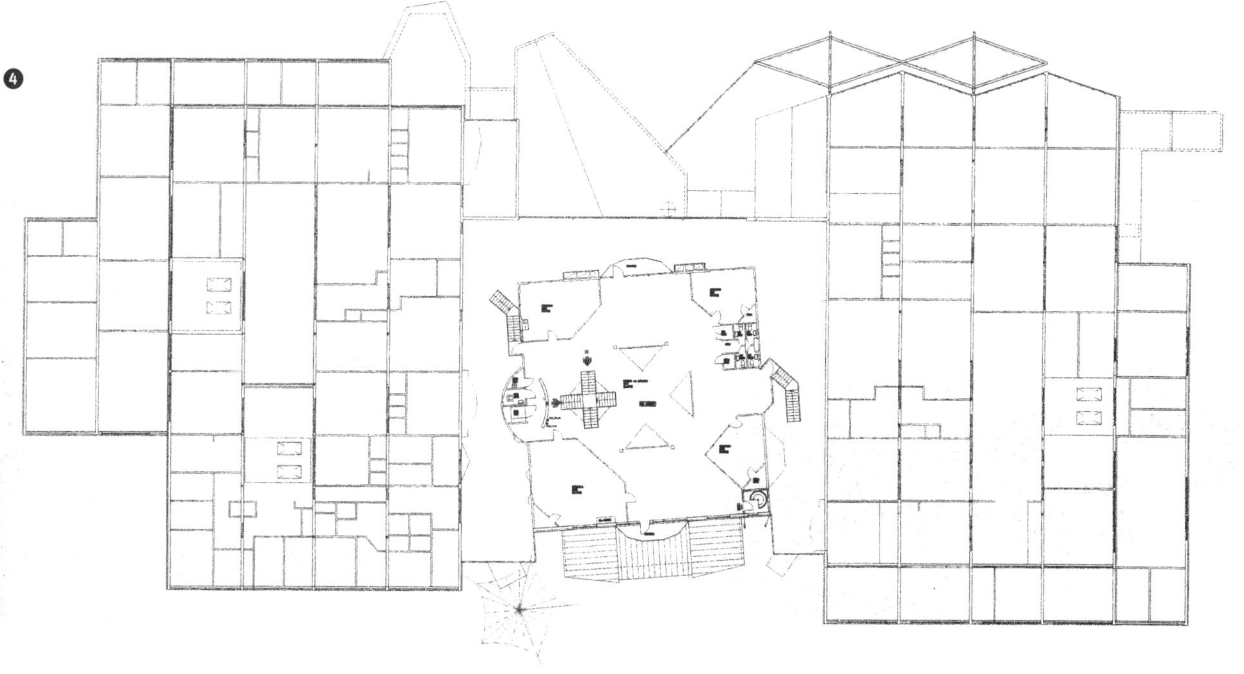

ARCHITECT
Viau Bergeron Architectes

TYPE OF SCHOOL
Vocational education and training

NO. OF STUDENTS
400

AGE RANGE
19 to 22 years

TYPE OF PROJECT
Extension

YEAR OF COMPLETION
1997

CLIENT
Commission scolaire de Laval

Although used for vocational training since 1972, a decision was taken to completely revamp the east wing of the Georges-Vanier educational complex when it became the home of a new institution, École Polymécanique de Laval, in the mid 1990s. The school offers courses in industrial mechanics and building trades to young people and adults in the greater Montreal area and, for some programmes, to the whole of Quebec.

The building has been extensively renovated and the new design emphasises the school's connection with building services. As one enters the school, windows open onto the workshops and laboratories. Bold open ceilings display the building's pipework and electrical and mechanical systems.

The interior plan and internal decoration attempts to establish a working atmosphere – offering functionality and free, unhampered movement between facilities – while encouraging social interaction. The main north-south thoroughfare leads to the centre of the building where functional areas including a shop and washrooms are situated. To the south the corridor is punctuated by natural light wells which mark out the junctions, emphasising them as natural meeting points. The area where it crosses the east–west thoroughfare opens up on to the first floor and its light well. This enhances the importance of the hub of the school; a place where all can meet and from where the city can be seen.

Places where people gather, such as the cafeteria, teachers' sitting room, staircases and administrative buildings, are located on the south side of the building. Large windows take advantage of the generous sunlight and the views across the des Prairies river towards Montreal.

Externally, two new entrances have been added on the east side. The choice of materials for the façades has been influenced by the style of the adjacent school so that the complex is integrated visually. But it is also important that students should feel that the new building is their own, and the south and east façades are punctuated by distinctive architectural markers indicating points of exterior movement and acting as signs for points of access.

1

2

3

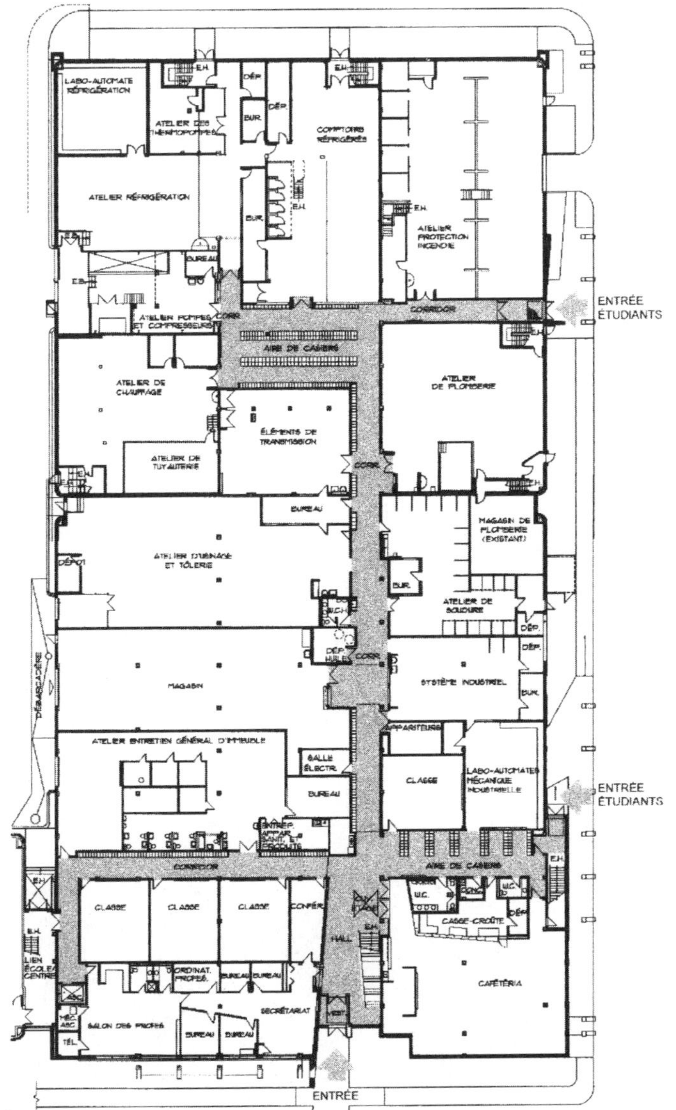

4

5

① *Open ceilings in the laboratories are designed to underline the importance of electrical and mechanical systems in buildings.*

② *The cafeteria and other common rooms are on the south side of the building, offering views across to Montreal in the distance.*

③ *The external façade blends visually with the adjoining school, but contains exuberant architectural detailing.*

④ *The plan of the ground floor which, for practical purposes, accommodates many of the industrial workshops and heavy equipment.*

⑤ *Open, well-lit corridors allow easy movement around the college and provide meeting places for students.*

ARCHITECT
ITIS Architects Sàrl

TYPE OF SCHOOL
Pre-school and primary education

NO. OF STUDENTS
310

AGE RANGE
4 to 12 years

TYPE OF PROJECT
New building and renovation

YEAR OF COMPLETION
1999

CLIENT
Commune de Neyruz Fribourg

Situated centrally and serving as a point of reference and convergence for village life, the renovation and extension of Neyruz primary school called for great sensitivity. The objective was to integrate and improve the existing amenities while adding new space that, through a flexible layout, could accommodate a variety of teaching methods, such as workshops and group work.

Imposing in its dimensions, the existing building retains a central position within the new complex. The areas for primary teaching and pre-school activities have been organised as two new blocks, allowing infant and nursery level children to become accustomed to the school before going on to primary level in the "big building".

The main entrance has been remodelled to function as both a reception and meeting area, avoiding the need to invest in a special facility for public events. The positioning of the extension, and skylights set within the ceilings, ensure that the new facilities are well lit without glare, and help maintain a constant temperature within the school.

Particular attention has been devoted to the various possibilities for computer usage, within the specific context of a village school. Every class also has access to networked computer facilities, offering each pupil the opportunity to exploit and explore modern communication methods. The reference library, together with its multimedia collections and facilities, is available for use by residents of Neyruz and neighbouring villages. Enriched with its new buildings and facilities, the school now hopes to become the centre of village social life.

1

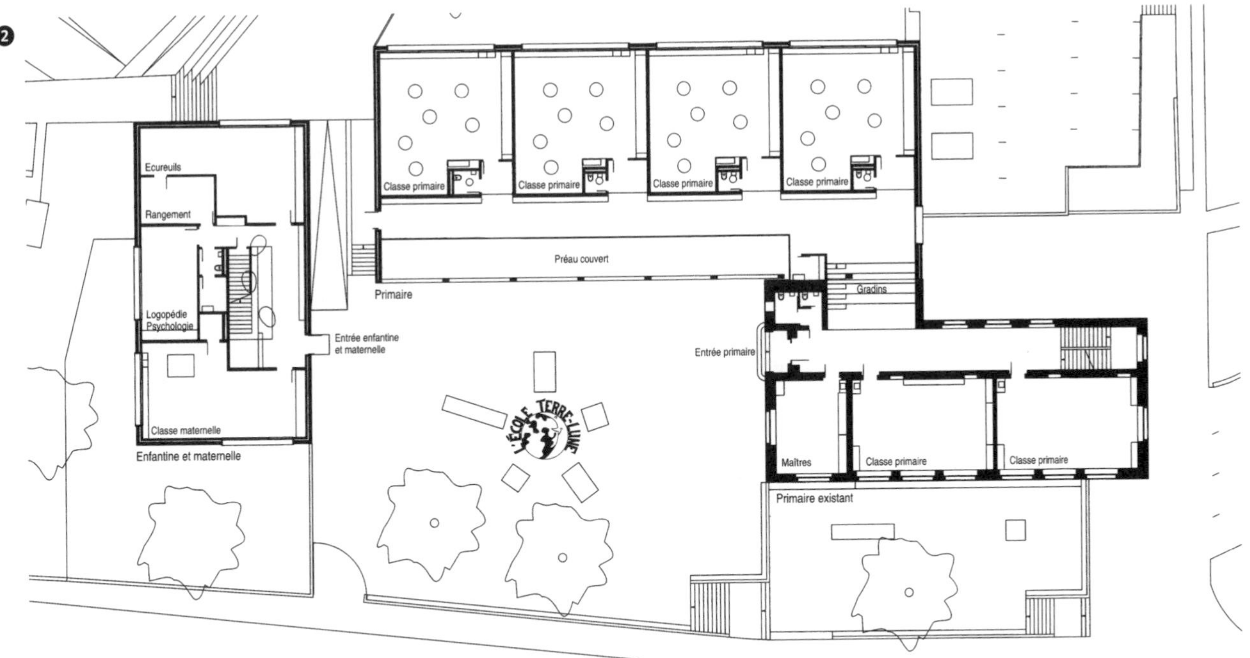

① *The new, yellow-fronted infants and primary blocks produce a striking contrast to the imposing original primary school building.*

② *Ground floor plan; the pre-school infants are housed in a separate block (left) from the main primary school.*

③ *Corridor in the new primary block, with a view out to the playground, with its sheltered portico, and the main entrance to the primary school.*

④ *View from the rear, with the infants school (right) and the new primary classrooms (left) in front of the old school building.*

⑤ *One of the light and airy classrooms in the new primary school extension.*

ARCHITECT
O'Donnell and Tuomey Architects

TYPE OF SCHOOL
Primary education

NO. OF STUDENTS
250

AGE RANGE
4 to 12 years

TYPE OF PROJECT
New building

YEAR OF COMPLETION
1998

CLIENT
Dept. of Education and Science/Ranelagh Multi-denominational School Association

The terraces and squares around this new school retain Dublin's original Georgian urban design. The architects have made conscious efforts to be sensitive to the environment, ensuring that the scale and character of the school is in keeping with the urban setting.

Set on a confined site, the design brief was to retain some of the atmosphere of the old school – demolished to make way for the new building – yet create a modern facility without the isolated classrooms of old. In the new school, teaching areas are arranged within a single two-storey linear building. They are organised like houses, each with a separate identity and separated by courtyards, and in sympathy with the domestic scale of the surrounding streets. Balconies between the teaching areas allow light and ventilation as well as helping to cut down traffic noise from the road. To maximise space, a roof terrace over the general purpose room can be used for occasional group work and supervised play.

An airy corridor runs along the main playground. The zone is intended as more than just a thoroughfare and accommodates ample seating, notice boards, coat hooks and drinking fountains. This area has a south-facing aspect onto the playground, but is sheltered from the sun and afforded privacy by canopy roofs and louvres.

The playground is landscaped to provide visual continuity of open space. Semi-mature trees have been planted to blend with the wooded gardens to the east and west of the school. A variety of other plants have been selected to enhance the environment and to provide educational opportunities for the pupils.

1

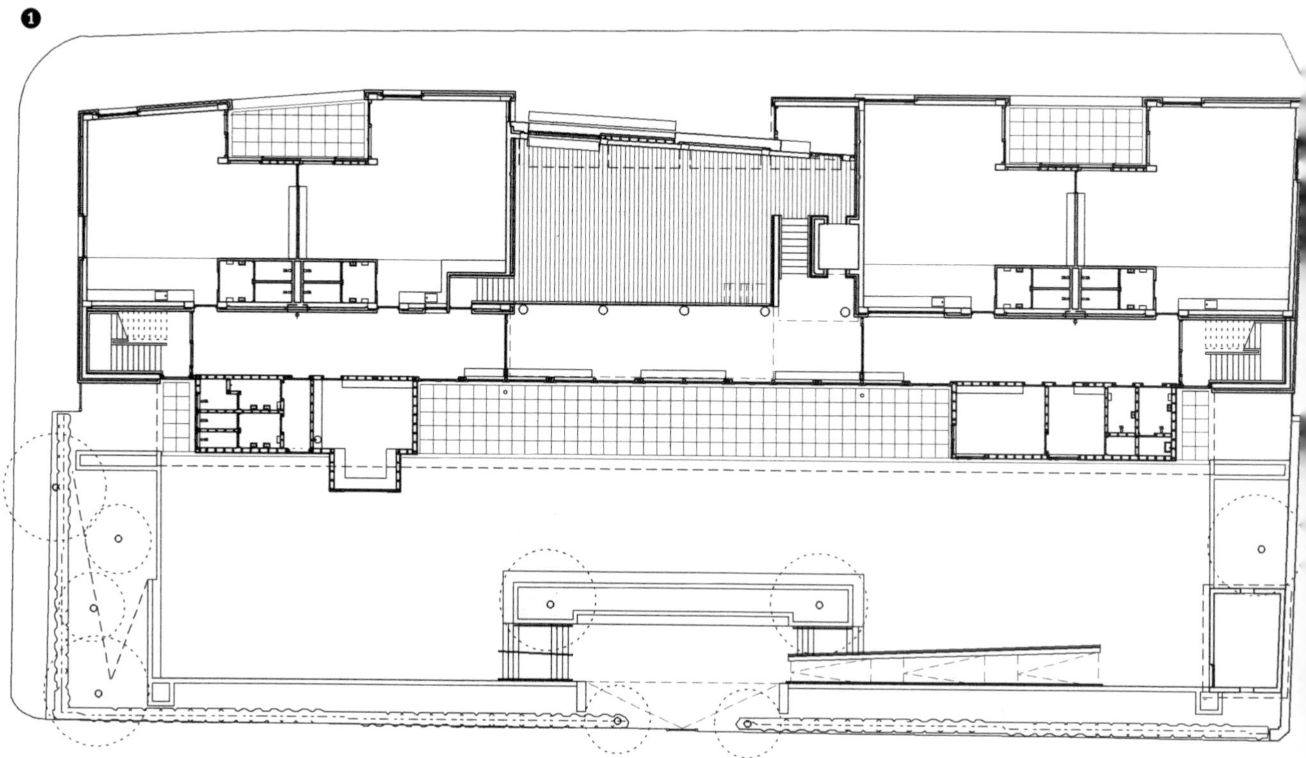

The building has been faced with salvaged brick and cut stone, obtained from a demolished building elsewhere in the city, to complement the Georgian houses. The pitched roofs are finished in terne-coated steel. Both internal and external materials have been chosen for their durability – they will need little or no maintenance. Externally, materials have been chosen for their ability to weather naturally.

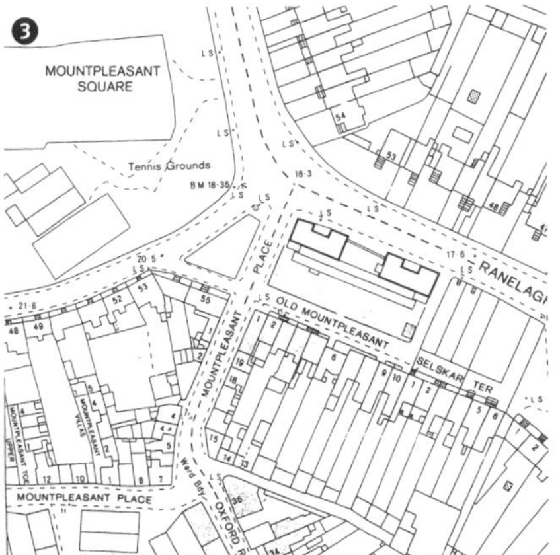

① *Ground floor plan; the school entrance leads into the playground. The classrooms are at the rear of the school running off an airy corridor.*

② *Interiors have concrete ceilings, plywood fittings and are decorated in warm earth colours.*

③ *The site plan.*

④ *The main corridor.*

⑤ *Children enter the school under the south-facing verandah from the sunken playground.*

Photographs courtesy of Denis Gilbert

ARCHITECT
Claudio Sargosa

TYPE OF SCHOOL
Primary, secondary and adult education

NO. OF STUDENTS
100

AGE RANGE
5 to 18+ years

TYPE OF PROJECT
New building

YEAR OF COMPLETION
1996

CLIENT
Ing. Massimo Ascolii

The Environmental Education Laboratory is situated in an area known as the Colline Metallifere – the "Metalliferous Hills" – an area of mining and metal production within Maremma Toscana. There are several parks and wildlife reserves, and the land has remained rich in natural habitats. The laboratory is set in eight hectares of Mediterranean forest. The aim of the laboratory is to make young people more aware of environmental issues and to understand how human activity and government policy can affect the environment in their local area.

The centre's social and educational programmes cater for groups of school children and adults. Each programme lasts up to five days and there is accommodation on site for up to 100 people. Emphasis is placed on practical activity and group work, which can involve participation in local projects such as recycling plants.

Facilities include three classrooms equipped with tables and chairs suited to the age and stature of the pupils, projectors and information technology. There are two laboratories. One is a technological laboratory with an instructional foundry, equipment for archaeology and restoration, as well as scale models illustrating how mining and metal processing techniques were developed in the region. The science laboratory contains smaller-scale equipment like microscopes and facilities for chemistry.

The largest room of the centre serves as both a library and an auditorium. With room for 120 people and equipped with projectors and sound and video systems, it is used for meetings and conferences

1

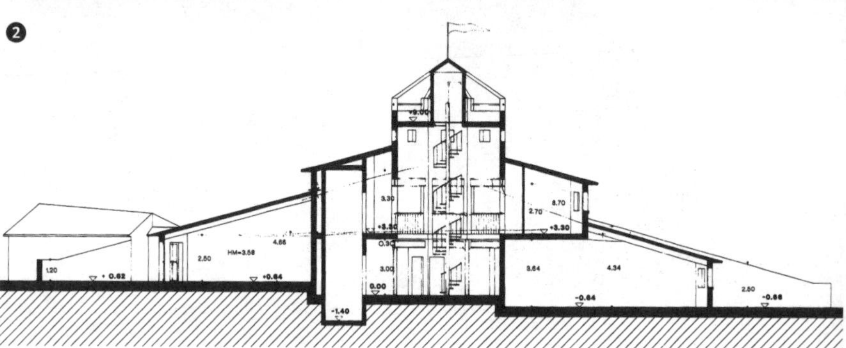
2

and as a lecture hall for larger groups. The library houses over 5 000 volumes on environmental issues. Other resources in the centre, such as a natural science collection, an aquarium and a herbarium, have been developed by the pupils using material collected during excursions.

The Environmental Educational Laboratory makes good use of the school grounds as a learning resource. There are four outdoor classrooms, a botanical garden, an excavation area which can be used to practice archaeological techniques and a plant nursery. There is also an eight-hectare wood in which field work can take place.

For students on residential courses, there are facilities for physical education and a restaurant serving meals made from organic produce.

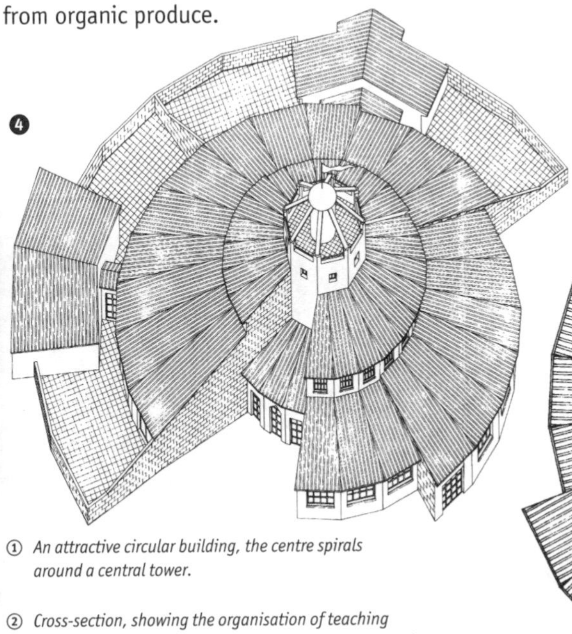

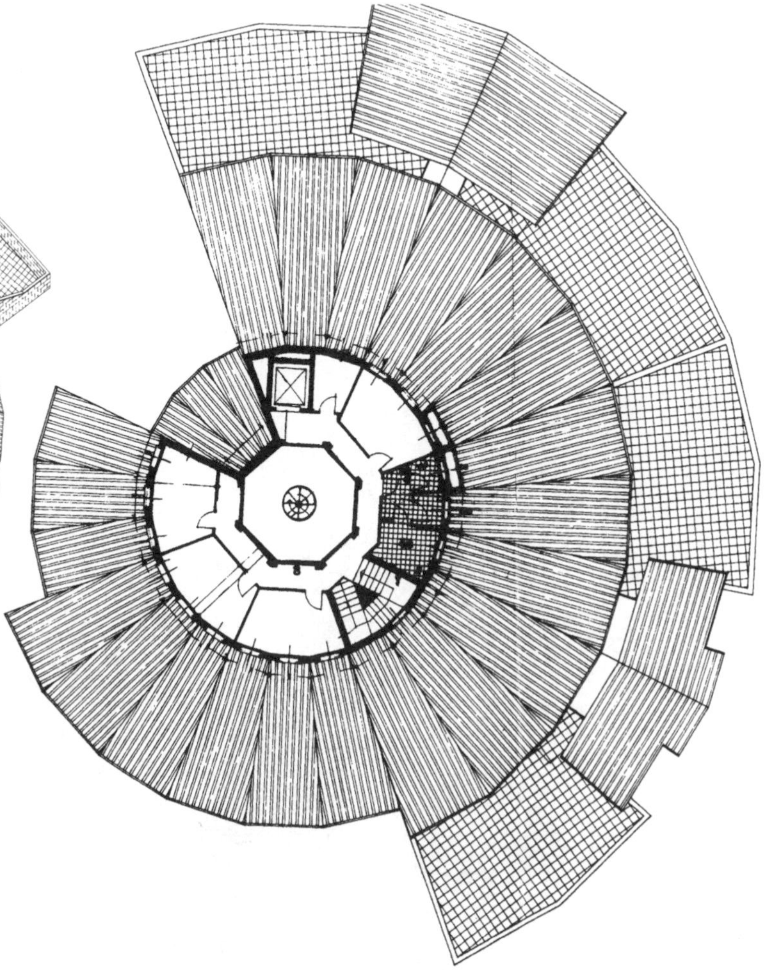

① An attractive circular building, the centre spirals around a central tower.

② Cross-section, showing the organisation of teaching rooms and laboratories around the central stairway and circulation space.

③ Housing the library, the 120-capacity auditorium provides a room for meetings, conferences and lectures as well as for individual study.

④ Drawings showing the distinctive character of the centre, including the four outside courtyards which are used for classes and group work.

ARCHITECT
Roberto Mariottini and Michele Mariottini

TYPE OF SCHOOL
Primary, secondary and adult education

NO. OF STUDENTS
Up to 50

AGE RANGE
8 to 19+ years

TYPE OF PROJECT
Renovation

YEAR OF COMPLETION
1998

CLIENT
Raoul Fiordiponti

The Asqua Centre for Environmental Education is situated in the Foresto Casentinesi National Park in Tuscany. It occupies a former forestry building, once used as offices and lodgings by forestry workers. Preserving the fabric of the building, it has been transformed into an educational centre that illustrates how respect for the environment can be compatible with acceptable living standards in the twenty-first century.

The building embodies principles of low energy consumption and environmental sustainability. It is constructed from local stone and has been externally finished with lime-based plaster. Other materials used are wood and brick. The heating system runs on a liquid propane gas thermal system and also uses energy recovered from the oven and fireplaces. Electrical systems are low-consumption and are partly powered by a hydroelectric turbine. Both tutors and participants are responsible for organising the separation and collection of waste material.

Running courses devoted to the study and protection of wildlife and the environment, Asqua has rooms and dormitories to accommodate up to 30 people. The centre offers participants an opportunity to engage in a variety of environmental educational projects, involving fieldwork and the collection and interpretation of data. These are tailored to the needs of a wide range of learners, from primary school children to postgraduate students, together with school teachers and professionals in environmental studies and eco-tourism.

Run by a management association affiliated to the National Association for the Environment (Legambiente), the Asqua centre has been supported by local and regional government, the Foreste Casentinesi National Park, the Ministry of Agriculture and Forestry, the National Forestry Corps and the Mountain Community (Comunita Montana del Casentino).

① *Students participate in a research project to capture and mark birds.*

② *The Asqua centre is housed in a former forestry workers' buiding in the heart of the national park.*

③ *The main living and study area.*

④ *Dining room, which doubles as a seminar room outside meal times.*

⑤ *Part of the canal which channels water to the hydroelectric turbine.*

⑥ *Ground floor plan following restoration; the centre installed wash and toilet facilities and environmentally friendly systems.*

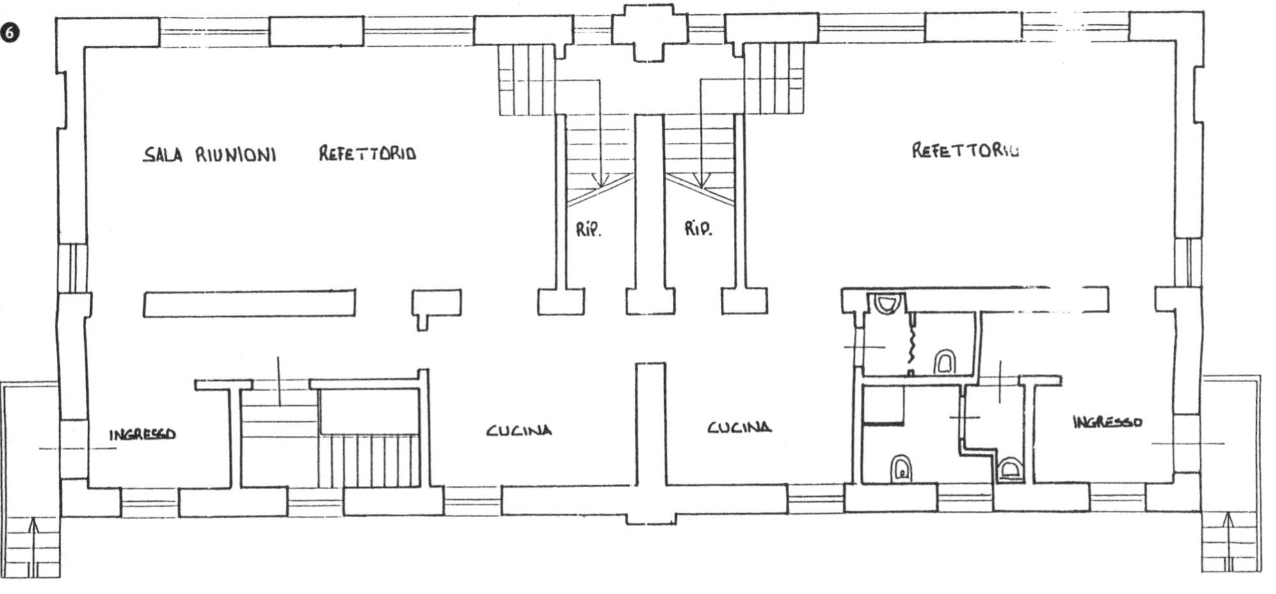

ARCHITECT
Parade Architekten

TYPE OF SCHOOL
Secondary education

NO. OF STUDENTS
1 280

AGE RANGE
10 to 19 years

TYPE OF PROJECT
New building

YEAR OF COMPLETION
1998

CLIENT
City of Wuppertal

The green belt along the river Wupper, where the school is situated, is a reclaimed former industrial area. The school is set beside a long tree-lined park that follows the path of a former railway along the river bank.

The heart of the school is a long glass-encased hall which connects all the rooms. This acts as the meeting place of the school, and is designed to encourage social interaction. The recreational area within the hall reflects the patterns of nature in the surrounding environment. It gives views of the ponds surrounding the school building and the suspension railway, the main landmark of Wuppertal.

The hall effectively separates the building in two: the southern part is dedicated to social and physical activities and contains the recreational and sports halls and the dining room, while the main classrooms are located in the northern area.

Appropriately, giving its setting, the school's design reflects environmental and ecological concerns. The extensive south-facing windows of the hall flood the school with natural light. They help heat the building in winter through passive solar energy. The hall contains a great number of plants, bushes and orchids, which as well as contributing to the attractiveness and relaxed atmosphere of the environment, provide shade and oxygen. In summer the surrounding ponds help to cool the building naturally. The flat "green roofs" of the dining hall, library and sports hall collect water and drain any surfeit into the ponds.

The school presents an open face to the public: the dining hall – a meeting place for pupils and teachers at lunchtime – is also used in the evening by local residents for performances, discussions, and meetings of clubs and societies.

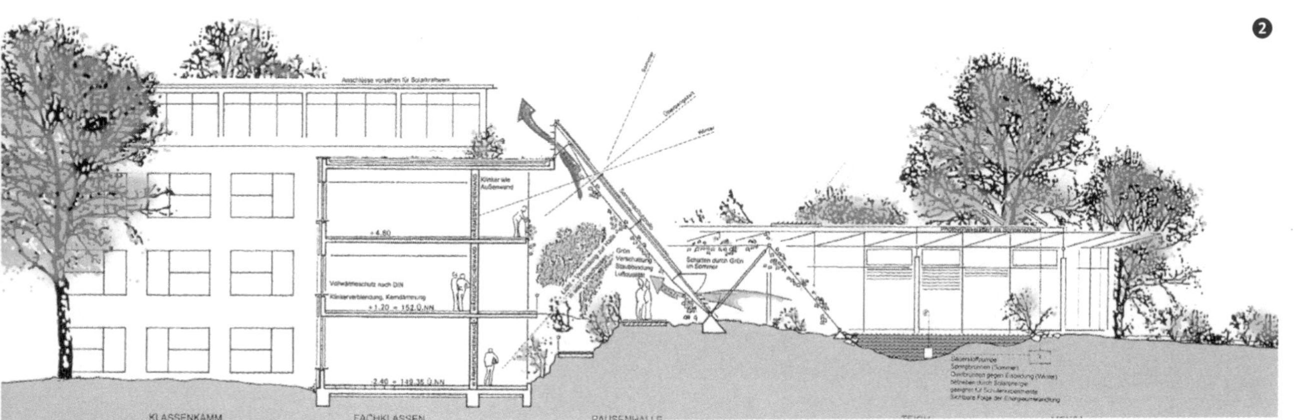

① *Ponds surround the school, providing an attractive feature and a place for students to relax.*

② *The glass-encased hall, the main spine of the school, provides an abundance of natural light and is energy efficient as it can be heated and cooled naturally.*

③ *Extensive use of glass presents an open and welcoming façade to pupils and public.*

④ *The hall is bedecked in plants, bushes and orchids, creating a welcoming and informal environment.*

⑤ *Students like to meet and chat in the hall.*

ARCHITECT
Chan Young Park

TYPE OF SCHOOL
Upper secondary education

NO. OF STUDENTS
1 180

AGE RANGE
16 to 19 years

TYPE OF PROJECT
New building

YEAR OF COMPLETION
1999

CLIENT
Chungnam Board of Education

Relocated from the city centre of Boryong, this high school has been built on the forested slopes of Mount Bong-Hwang. The local education board, alumni, school employees and the local community have all been involved in the planning and construction of the new school campus, providing an example of how different bodies can successfully co-operate in a project of this nature.

In order to reduce building costs and minimise environmental disturbance, the design and layout reflects the features of the existing topography and landscape, and the configuration of the buildings is well adapted to the contours of the site. The school is in harmony with its natural environment, and the landscaped grounds provide a splash of colour between the brick and stone buildings.

All buildings on the campus are linked by attractive glass-covered walkways. Each building is designed so that it has an individual identity and its own outside space, which gives the pupils views towards the wooded hills beyond.

A series of steps leads to the main entrance to the school. Two main blocks house the classrooms and science laboratories. The campus includes a gymnasium, library, music theatre, cafeteria, shop and activity rooms for student clubs. A plaza, used for outdoor activities, is situated between the classroom blocks. School facilities are open to the public, both for recreation and lifelong learning.

To support curriculum development, there is a seminar room and six curriculum research labs to encourage teachers to exchange ideas and discuss common problems. A multipurpose 350-seater room is used for parents meetings and as a forum for guest speakers to the school.

1

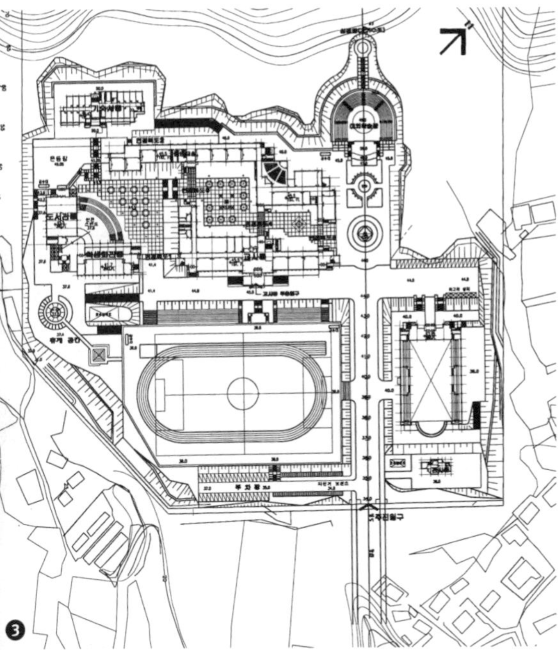

① *The school has been relocated to a green field site at the edge of Boryong.*

② *Attractive pink brick façades provide a contrast with the dark forest setting.*

③ *The site plan; the school has dormitory blocks for boarding students and extensive sports facilities.*

④ *Entrance hall inside one of the classroom blocks.*

⑤ *Glass-covered aerial walkways link main classroom blocks on the campus.*

ARCHITECT
Parade Architekten

TYPE OF SCHOOL
Secondary, tertiary and adult education

NO. OF STUDENTS
700

AGE RANGE
18+ years

TYPE OF PROJECT
Extension

YEAR OF COMPLETION
1994

CLIENT
Land North Rhine Westphalia and private industry

Given that this vocational college runs courses in glass, ceramics, and art and design, and has close connections with the glass industry, it is perhaps not surprising that glass is used extensively in the design of Staatliches Berufskolleg Rheinbach. The innovative use of glass in conjunction with steel and a protective metal skin demonstrates the technical possibilities of the material to students and, perhaps, may inspire future projects.

The main buildings have an elliptical shape, with the entrance, halls and foyer a continuation of the other rooms. Inside, the glass walls offer perspectives at all levels, vertically and horizontally, with views both to the planted courtyard and the more informal landscapes of the college grounds.

Although the building is technically advanced, the design accords high priority to ecological aspects. It demonstrates how educational facilities can be integrated with the surrounding landscape and be energy efficient. The glass façade of the main building is south facing to make maximum use of solar energy: both passively through direct sunlight and actively through photovoltaic plates. The college's microclimate is stabilised by a low, partly green roof in one section of the

1

2

building, the many plants inside the building and the large "eco pond".

The college is wired for the twenty-first century. Students have access to modern communication and information technology in CAD rooms and the main craft workshops. The graphic design and media department supports a range of multimedia technologies, with the latest software for film cutting, audio-visual programmes, presentation and documentation facilities, and three-dimensional programmes.

Photographs courtesy of Ralph Richter

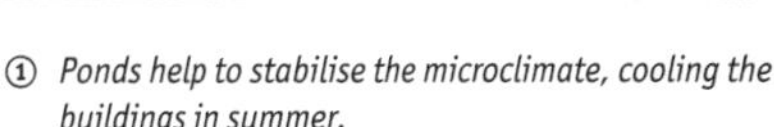

① *Ponds help to stabilise the microclimate, cooling the buildings in summer.*

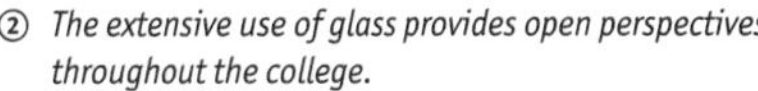

② *The extensive use of glass provides open perspectives throughout the college.*

③ *The college is a monument to glass, demonstrating its versatility as a building material.*

④ *An aerial shot illustrates the elliptical shape of the two main rows of college buildings.*

⑤ *The site and ground floor plan.*

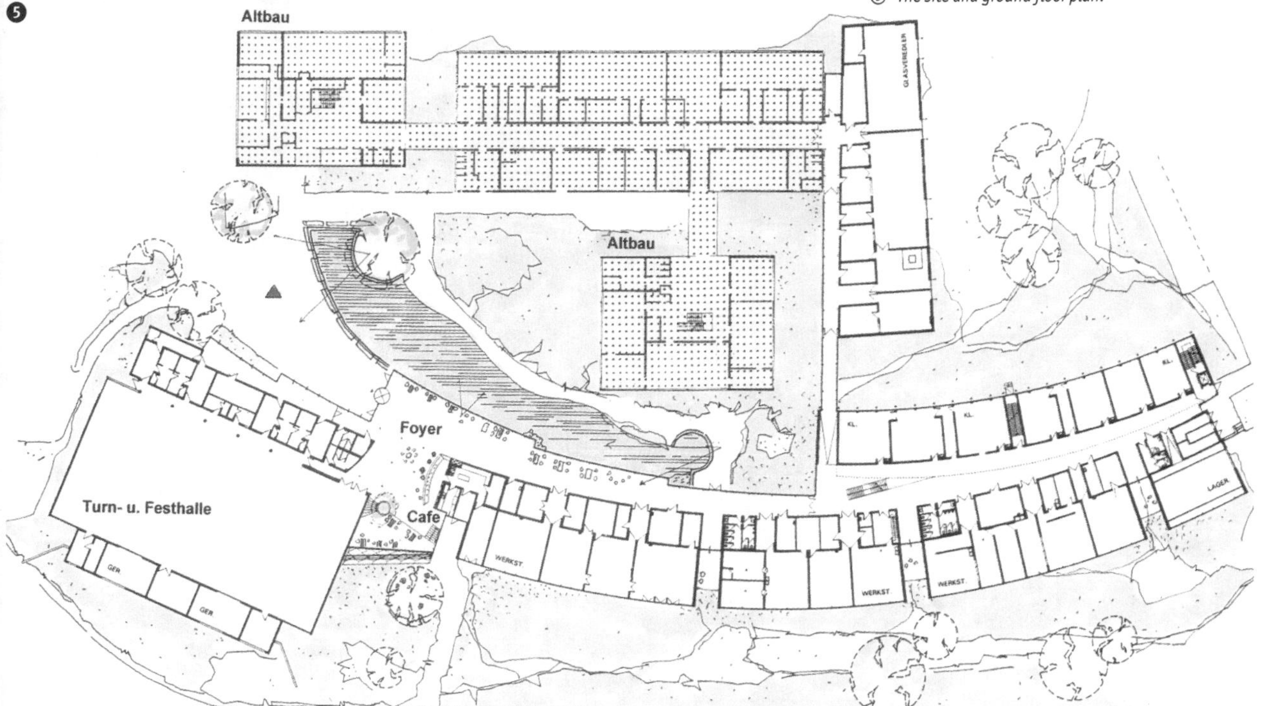

PEB

Chapter three

Tertiary Education – Coping with Demand

The tertiary education sector, including universities, other – sometimes highly specialised – institutions for higher study, and colleges of further education, is going through a period of very rapid change. Growth in student numbers, as tertiary education moves from an elite to a mass pursuit, together with an increase in the range and type of programmes on offer and the changing demands of students, many of whom are part-time adults, is leading to a fundamental reconsideration of the nature of facilities to be provided. Technological developments and the emergence of a global market for tertiary education pose even greater challenges.

The colleges and universities which have been selected for inclusion in this chapter seek to address through their design one or more of these developments. In several cases this is manifested primarily through a change of role for the library and resource centre. Historically thought to be the "centre" of tertiary education, the library is changing with developments in information technology, teaching and learning methods, and changes in society. Coupled with budget pressures, demands for expansion and increased expenditures, the maintenance of library services requires an examination of new methods of delivery and use.

In the knowledge-based society, a more diversified and more business-like approach is being taken. And in the face of rising numbers, limited resources and raised expectations of service and quality, there is increasing pressure on managers for efficiency and accountability.

The impact of competition, notably from the private for-profit sector, linked to the growing use of information technology for course delivery, raises real questions about the nature of the facilities institutions will require, particularly the need to provide for flexibility and adaptability to meet short-term and long-term changing demand.

ARCHITECT
ARK-House Architects Ltd

TYPE OF SCHOOL
Tertiary education, adult education

NO. OF STUDENTS
600

AGE RANGE
18+ years

TYPE OF PROJECT
New building

YEAR OF COMPLETION
1999

CLIENT
Ministry of Education

The Corona Information Centre is a new building designed to widen access to the University of Helsinki's information services and maximise their educational effectiveness. By bringing together all the departmental libraries of the Viikki campus under one roof, the university can offer users longer opening hours and access to up-to-date information and learning technology.

Housing the Helsinki University's Viikki Science Library, with 8 000 metres of shelf space, the centre is Finland's largest scientific library in its field. Its information technology infrastructure connects it to other science libraries in Finland and abroad. This gives users access to inter-library services and central electronic sources of information.

As the main building of the Agriculture and Forestry Faculty, the centre incorporates administrative offices and teaching and assembly facilities. It also accommodates a bookshop, a café and a branch of the Helsinki University Press. In addition, Helsinki City Library has a branch within the Corona Centre.

Both the university science library and the city library are open to the public,

1

2

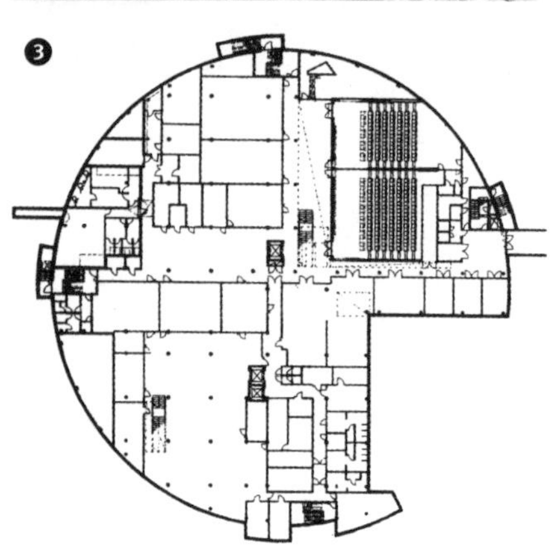
3

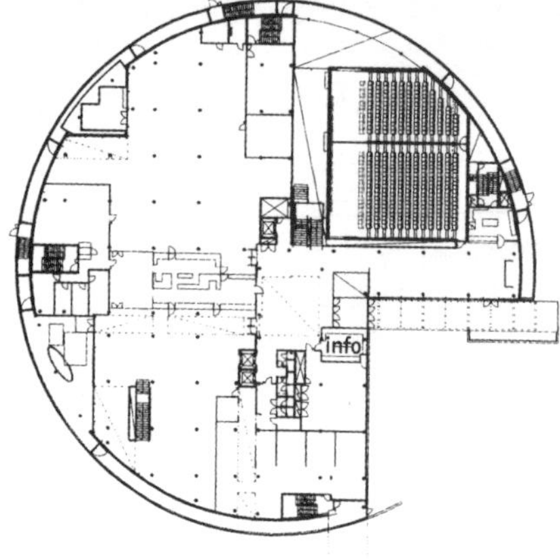

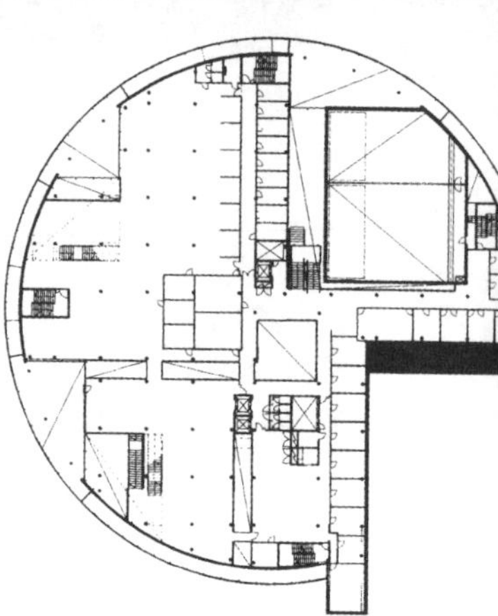

and there is a common reader service area, reference section and reading room. The city library supports the science library through the acquisition of non-specialist books dealing with subjects of interest to the students, lecturers and researchers of Helsinki University.

The building's glazed exterior requires little maintenance and supports an efficient air-conditioning system. Its curved façade is designed to reflect an open and holistic approach to education and inspired the name Corona.

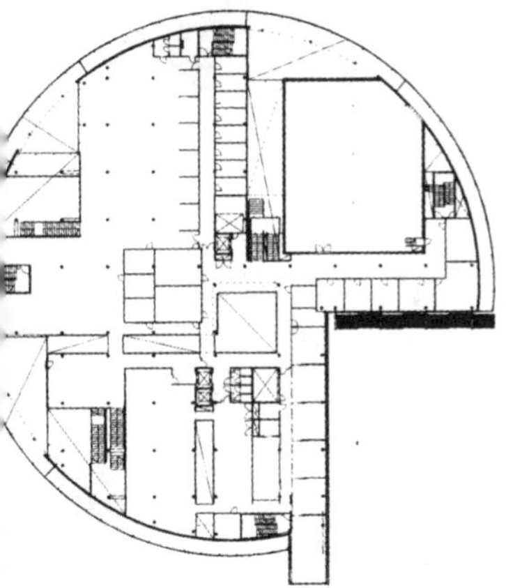

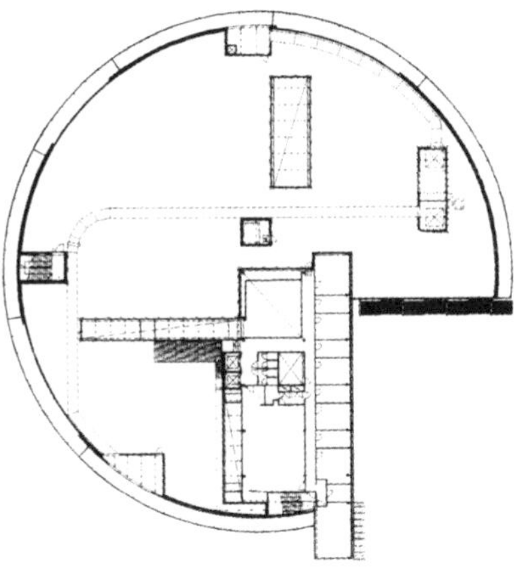

① *The imposing main entrance hall.*

② *With its striking curved façade, the Corona Centre looks dramatic both day and night.*

③ *Floor plans (from basement, far left, to third floor, right) show the unusual circular plan of the centre.*

④ *One of the internal gardens and communal areas.*

⑤ *The cafeteria, which is open to all users of the building.*

⑥ *In addition to the library, the centre also houses offices, a conference room and two lecture theatres.*

ARCHITECT
Murray O'Laoire Architects

TYPE OF SCHOOL
Tertiary education

NO. OF STUDENTS
16 525

AGE RANGE
18+ years

TYPE OF PROJECT
New building

YEAR OF COMPLETION
1998

CLIENT
Dept. of Education and Science/University of Limerick

Designed to accommodate up to 1 100 users at any one time, the library and information services building forms one side of the forecourt to the University of Limerick campus. Opened in 1998, the new building seeks to integrate a traditional library with the needs of a modern learning and teaching facility.

The architects have designed a building that reflects the way that university members actually use library and information technology services for teaching, learning and research. They have created a building that provides a variety of well-related working and storage environments.

A central spine provides the main book storage area, with capacity to store 500 000 volumes. "Fingers", running perpendicularly from the spine, contain the reader areas and study rooms. Between the fingers, there are two atria which ensure that all parts of the four-storey building receive natural light and ventilation.

All desks are designed (and wired) for book study and Internet research. There are also several group rooms which can be configured for tutorials, lectures, discussions and distance learning. There are graphics, photographic and audiovisual studios for multimedia work

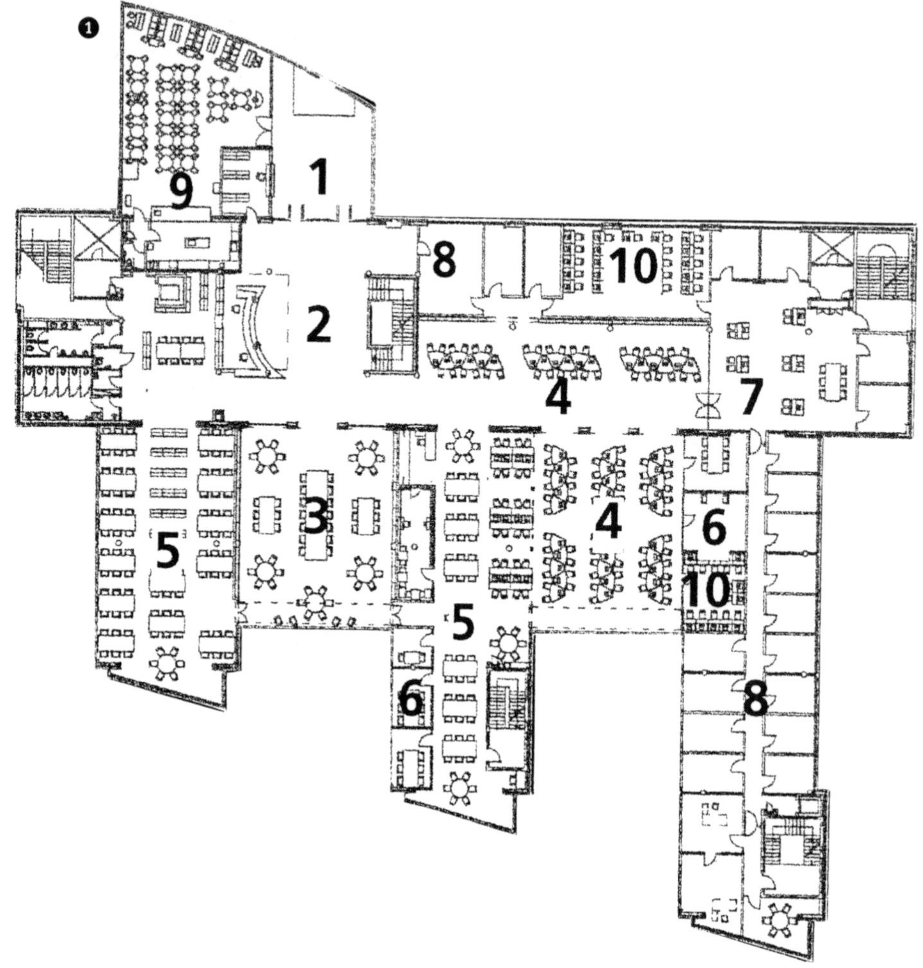

and training suites to support information skills programmes. The component grids and servicing routes are designed to accommodate future technological developments, and projected increases in demand – as student numbers increase – can be met by the addition of another "finger" to the building.

The design conserves energy usage by making full use of natural ventilation, daylight, solar control and thermal massing. Externally, the centre blends well with the university campus by drawing on features from the existing buildings, using dark brick, expansive dark glazing, and exposed copper and brickwork surfaces.

① *The ground floor plan; the desks in the atrium and spine (4) allow Internet access; other general reader areas (5) and group study rooms (6) are in the fingers.*

② *A view of the study area in one of the library's two atria.*

③ *Stairwells linking the floors at the end of the spine provide a splash of colour.*

④ *The glass-fronted atria ensure the reader areas are bathed in natural light.*

⑤ *The external façades comprise brick walls and expansive dark glazing.*

⑥ *The end of each finger is extensively glazed, providing a further source of natural light.*

Photographs courtesy of Eamon O'Mahony

ARCHITECT
Atelier PRO

TYPE OF SCHOOL
Tertiary education

NO. OF STUDENTS
1600

AGE RANGE
17 to 23 years

TYPE OF PROJECT
New building

YEAR OF COMPLETION
1996

CLIENT
Haagse Hogeschool, University of Professional Education

By the 1980s, the industrial area around Laakhaven, a harbour in The Hague, had been in decline for many years and it was virtually isolated from the rest of the city. The Haagse Hogeschool, an institute for higher professional education, has been built on the site as part of an ambitious urban regeneration plan.

Bordered by water on three sides, the Haagse Hogeschool has three main buildings laid out imaginatively in the confined site. A curving high block acts as a link between the railway station, the waterfront and the other college buildings. This connects with a lower linear block and an oval building which contains the college's auditorium and large lecture rooms. To create a sense of connectivity, the designers have planned cycle routes and pathways through the site and kept clear sightlines to urban landmarks.

The Hogeschool utilises a wide range of spaces to meet its diverse requirements: lecture theatres, classrooms, workshops for practicals and booths for individual study. Additionally, teaching staff accommodation is situated next to teaching facilities, giving students easy access to individual teaching staff.

Through clever use of space, a wide range of study programmes can be offered on this single site. The faculties are close together, making it easier for students to select modules across disciplines and encouraging sharing of ideas and approaches between departments. This approach has resulted in four internal centres of expertise being set up to develop and implement educational innovations. Students are supported in their studies by state-of-the-art library and computer facilities.

1

① *The Hogeschool has a waterfront setting and, with offices, housing, cafes and restaurants, forms part of an extensive urban regeneration plan.*

② *A huge atrium forms the centre-piece of the oval building which accommodates lecture theatres, an auditorium and many faculty and staff offices.*

③ *The building looks spectacular at night.*

④ *Throughout the building there is a wide variety of spaces for studying and socialising.*

⑤ *The first floor plan showing the imaginative alignment of the three main college buildings.*

Photographs courtesy of Luuk Kramer

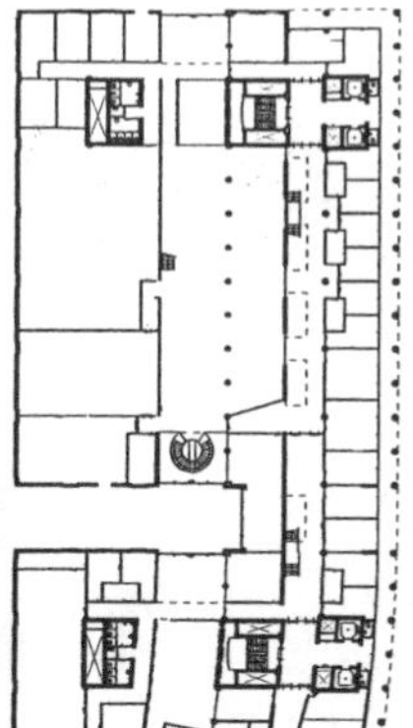

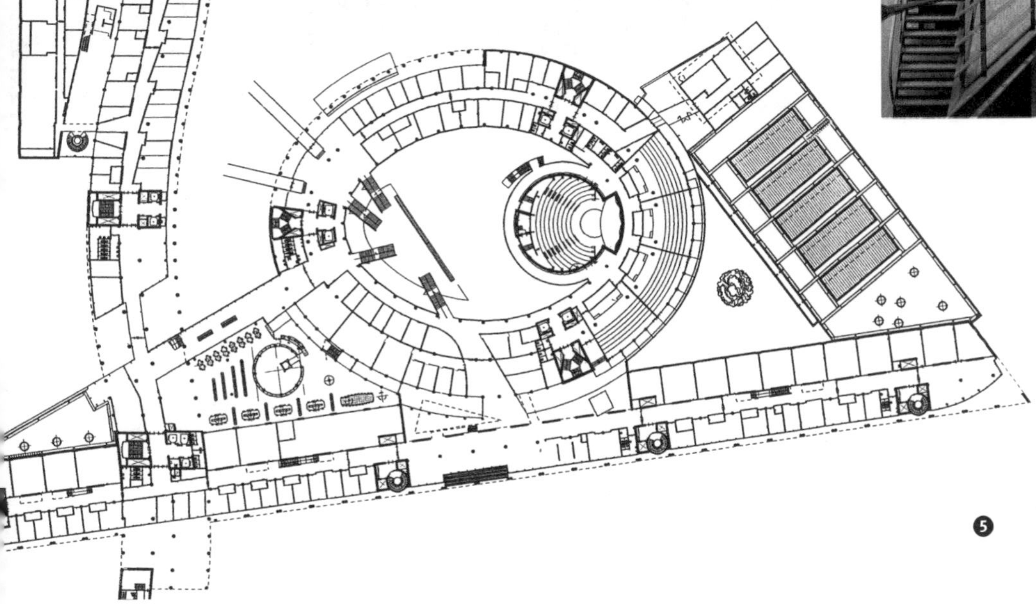

ARCHITECT
Günther Domenig and Hermann Eisenköck

TYPE OF SCHOOL
Tertiary education

NO. OF STUDENTS
14 000

AGE RANGE
18+ years

TYPE OF PROJECT
New building/extension

YEAR OF COMPLETION
1996

CLIENT
Bundesimmobilien-gesellschaft mbH (BIG)

Prior to the opening of this new faculty building, the 35 institutes of law and social sciences were scattered across the city of Graz. This did not make for easy collaboration between faculty members; there was little opportunity for chance encounters and spontaneous exchange of ideas. A further frustration was that the growing number of staff and students was putting the existing teaching and research facilities under enormous strain.

With 30 000 square metres of usable space, this new building is designed to resolve these problems. Known as the Resowi building – an acronym of the initials of the two faculties – it brings all law and social science institutes under one roof, enhancing the possibilities for joint projects and cross-departmental exchange. Teaching facilities have been expanded, with the addition of 11 new lecture rooms and seating in seminar halls for up to 4 000 students.

The specialist library, which brings together 800 000 books housed on 30 000 metres of shelf space, has greatly enhanced the university's research facilities. The library also has up-to-date multimedia facilities, with Internet workstations and access to other educational technologies.

In addition to the academic facilities, the building incorporates the kitchens, a café

1

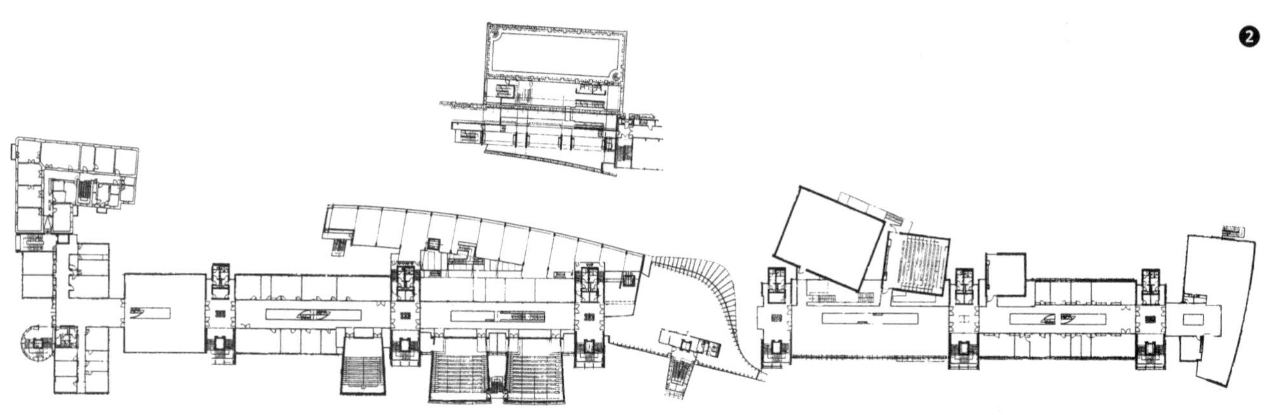
2

and a university shop. Outside, the narrow landscaped grounds and water features serve as a habitat for beetles, butterflies, grass, flowers, bushes and trees, which will be left to thrive naturally over the next few years. This will attract not only faculty members but also botanists, zoologists and tourists, transforming a university building into a social and cultural centre which can meet the diverse needs of the community.

Situated along a main road known as the alley of architecture, Resowi sits comfortably beside such architectural masterpieces as Klaus Kada's plant physiology building and Volker Giencke's greenhouses.

① *Plaza and entrances at the central point of the Resowi building.*

② *The first floor plan; the main lecture theatres are accessed from the first floor spine.*

③ *Curved and sloping glass elements add interest to the linear façades.*

④ *Atria spaced at intervals along the building ensure well-lit interiors, providing circulation spaces and breaking up the corridors.*

⑤ *The library is housed over several floors to provide room for study and some 800 000 volumes.*

⑥ *Façade showing protruding lecture halls.*

Photographs courtesy of Hermut Tezak

ARCHITECT
Bruno Albert, Camille Ghysen

TYPE OF SCHOOL
Tertiary education, adult education

NO. OF STUDENTS
1600

AGE RANGE
18 to 25 years

TYPE OF PROJECT
New building and renovation

YEAR OF COMPLETION
1994

CLIENT
Hautes Études Commerciales de Liège (HEC)

By the late 1980s, this expanding tertiary education establishment was housed in a series of dilapidated and often unsuitable buildings spread across Liège. It was decided to concentrate the institution on a single site and, contrary to prevailing trends, to look for a city centre site.

The plot that was chosen contains the remains of the medieval convent of Beauregard, which was in the process of being classified as an historic monument. Far from being an obstacle to the site's development, the town planning department welcomed the opportunity to secure the future of the convent building and the college obtained subsidies for the restoration and conservation work.

The reference library – which includes multimedia facilities – is now housed in the restored building, creating an interesting and unique setting for study. A sensitive blending of ancient buildings and contemporary architecture has been achieved. Access to the former convent is by way of a cloister and the new building, while not sacrificing its own qualities, is deliberately unassertive so as to ease the stylistic transition between old and new.

The main access to the institute is through an entrance on the rue Louvrex which dates back to the eighteenth century. On the ground floor are two main auditoria, the larger with 500 seats. These lie behind a large hall which acts as a reception, waiting and relaxation area.

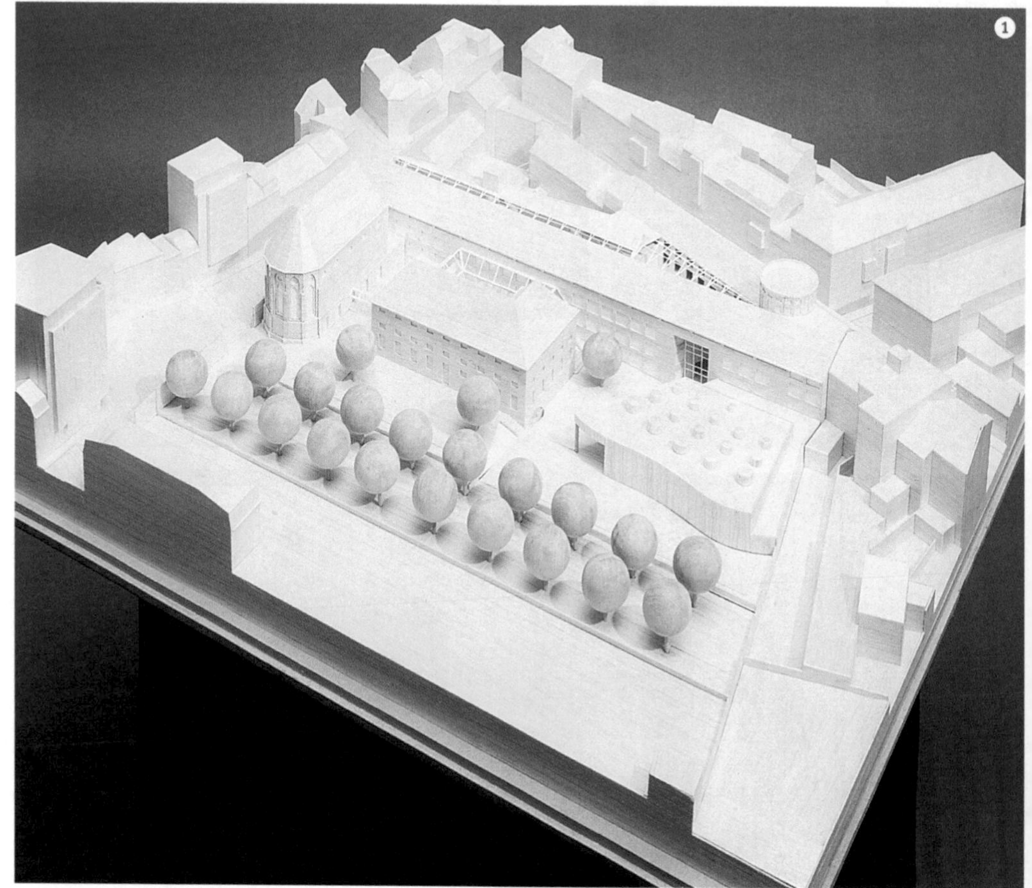

In the centre of the complex, all rooms and offices are situated in two wings. These two-storey blocks are separated by walkways, a patio and an interior "street" area which is covered by a glass roof. It is both a circulation space and a place where students can socialise.

With its city location, the college relies on the existing infrastructure of shops, restaurants, snack bars and public spaces, thereby alleviating the need to include these facilities within the complex and benefiting the local economy. This policy has given the institute enough space to accommodate future extensions and ensures mixing and interaction between students and the neighbourhood.

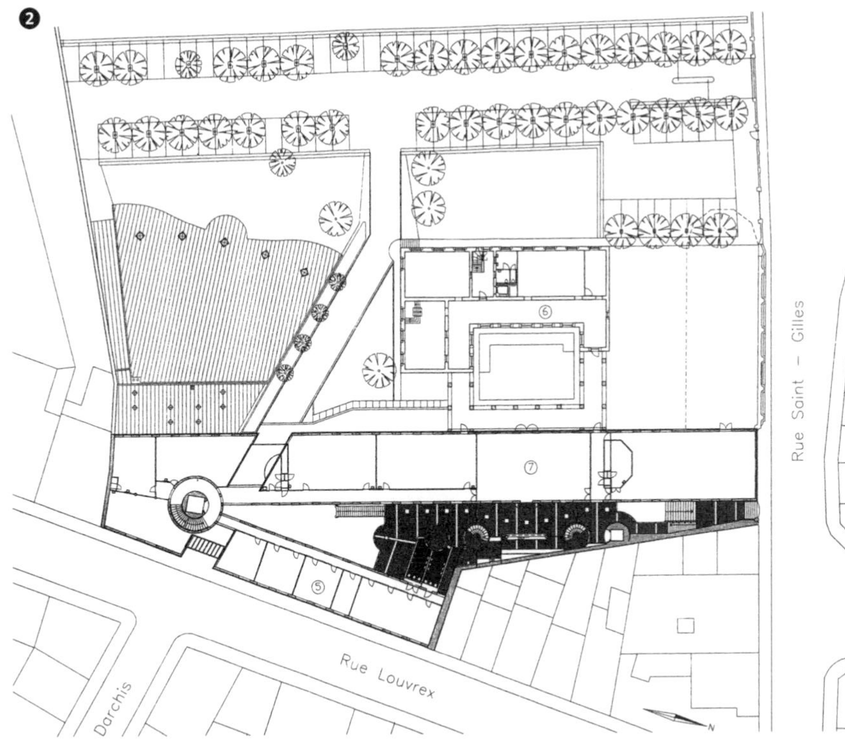

① *Architect's model of the campus, the seventeenth century convent in the foreground (to the left).*

② *The site plan; the library and resource centre (6), cafeteria (7) and offices (5) are marked.*

③ *A covered street, providing an attractive circulation space and meeting area, links the two wings housing the institute's offices and classrooms.*

④ *Sensitive additions have created a campus on a tight urban site, preserving the existing historical buildings.*

ARCHITECT
ABCP Architecture et Urbanisme, and Duclos Fournier, architectes

TYPE OF SCHOOL
Tertiary education

NO. OF STUDENTS
3 000

AGE RANGE
17+ years

TYPE OF PROJECT
Extension

YEAR OF COMPLETION
1998

CLIENT
Cégep de Saint-Hyacinthe

During the first half of the 1990s, the number of students at Cégep de Saint-Hyacinthe rose by 50 per cent from 2 000 to 3 000. To accommodate this influx of students, the infrastructure of the college has been expanded. In total, 12 000 square metres of extensions have been added to the original floor area of 35 500 square metres.

The challenge has been to build close enough to the central hub of the college, to ensure that the new accommodation is close to the main activities, and to do so without obstructing the windows of the existing building. The problem has been solved by linking three of the four extensions to the original building with five-metre-wide covered walkways, or galleria, to provide a break in this concentric development.

The galleria, and thus the outside of the original building, are well lit by windows at the ends of each section and by light wells in the roof, which also bring heat into the space and into the original building. The architectural elements of the extensions – the dimensions and the type and colour of the materials used – have all been chosen to blend in with the original building.

The galleria concept was developed by ABCP and it provides a network of thoroughfares and multipurpose public spaces. Furnished with tables, chairs and armchairs, they are designed to foster a sense of community. As well as providing a reception area for the academic departments and a site for displaying college information, the galleria are used for individual and group work. More importantly, they are a meeting point, somewhere to exchange ideas with friends and colleagues and to relax during meals and coffee breaks. Their use has helped alleviate overcrowding in the library and the cafeteria.

1

2

① *Reception area and information point at the entrance to one of the galleria.*

② *Providing a circulation space linking the extensions to the college, the galleria are used as a meeting point.*

③ *Aerial view; the college has links with business acting as a technology transfer centre for the textile industry.*

④ *Ground floor plan; the galleria (shaded) connect the new extensions (blocks K, J, H) to the original building.*

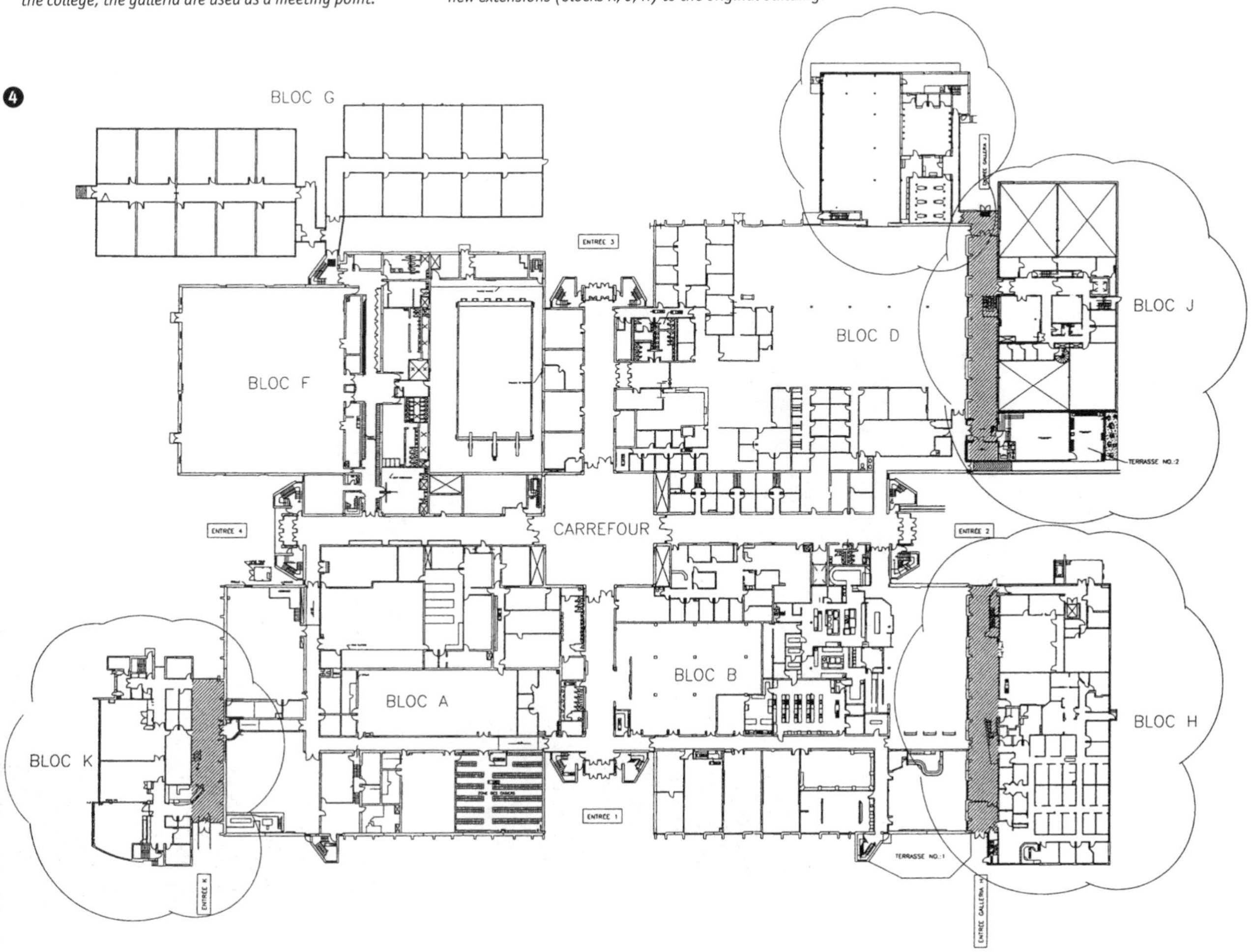

4

BLOC G

ENTRÉE 3

BLOC F

BLOC D

BLOC J

TERRASSE NO. 2

ENTRÉE 4

CARREFOUR

ENTRÉE 2

BLOC A

BLOC B

BLOC K

BLOC H

ENTRÉE 1

TERRASSE NO. 1

ENTRÉE K

ARCHITECT
Saucier + Perrotte/ Menkès Shooner Dagenais

TYPE OF SCHOOL
Tertiary education

NO. OF STUDENTS
1000

AGE RANGE
19+ years

TYPE OF PROJECT
Extension and renovation

YEAR OF COMPLETION
1999

CLIENT
Direction des Immeubles, Université de Montréal

The University of Montreal's Faculty of Planning brings together four design schools on the site of a former convent. The original H-shaped building has been expanded and enhanced with a new entrance and additional facilities. The use of steel and transparent glass structures to conserve, extend and modernise the existing stone building mirrors the urban design concepts that are being developed by the faculty's students.

The development programme provides an additional 4 000 square metres of studios and lecture halls, and another 1 900 square metres of renovations in the existing building. It also includes an ongoing scheme to put computer workstations into all workshops and link them up to an intranet.

The transparent rectangular structure located behind the former convent building connects the old to the new. It is designed to encourage creativity and the sharing of ideas. Work produced in the workshops is exhibited in this transparent space, providing ideas and inspiration for students and teachers across the different schools, enhancing the faculty's pedagogical principles which place great emphasis on shared training and inter-disciplinary communication.

The heart of the building is a 400-seat auditorium, built within the stripped volume of the original chapel. It can be transformed into two separate auditoriums by drawing screens across a balcony. This flexible use of facilities is replicated across the building; open plan studios can be divided with moveable screens. The aim is to create a variety of spaces of different scales, all with access to the latest teaching and learning technologies.

1

2

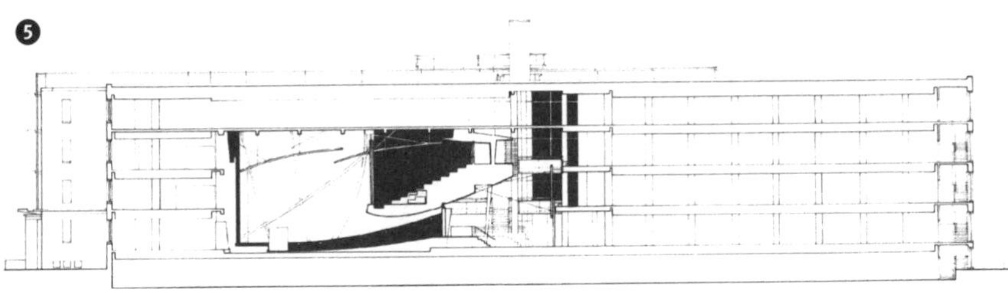

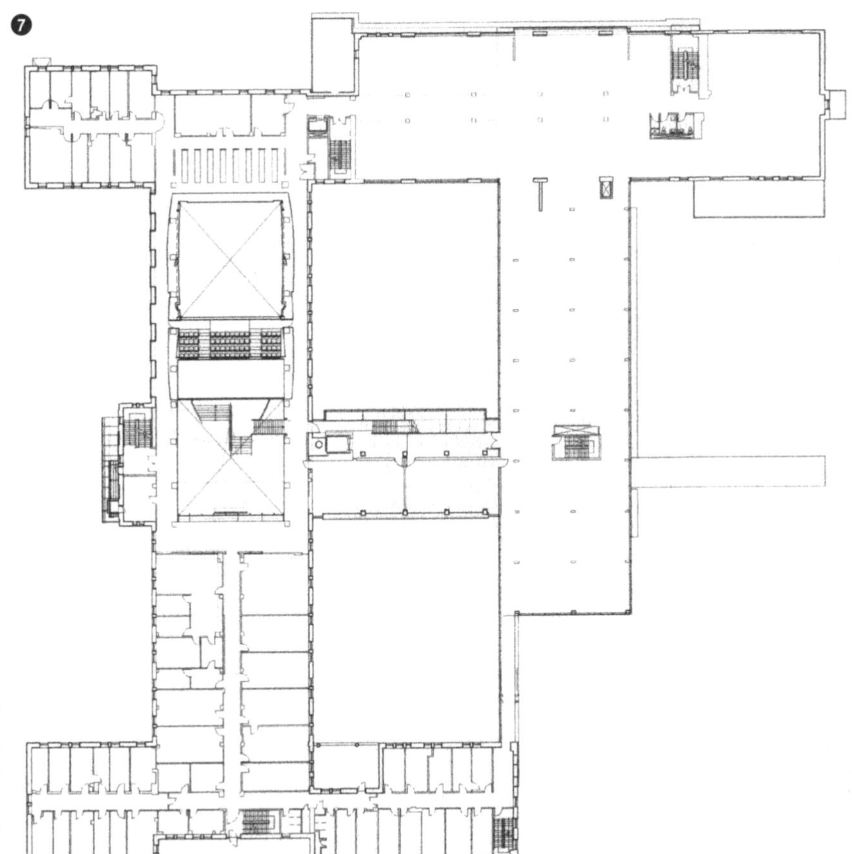

① *The façade of the existing building has been enhanced with corten panels and glazed curtain walls.*

② *Foyer hall behind the 400-seat auditorium.*

③ *Workshops in the studio wing, a modern extension to the old convent building.*

④ *Walkway leading from the park to the new studio wing.*

⑤ *Cross-section of the convent; the auditorium is located within the stripped volume of the original chapel.*

⑥ *Inside the main auditorium.*

⑦ *Second floor plan; the glass-fronted studio extension (right) intersects with the renovated existing building.*

ARCHITECT
Jim Coady & Associates

TYPE OF SCHOOL
Tertiary education

NO. OF STUDENTS
1462

AGE RANGE
18 to 22+ years

TYPE OF PROJECT
Extension

YEAR OF COMPLETION
1999

CLIENT
Dept. of Education and Science/Letterkenny Institute of Technology

In the past four years, Letterkenny Institute of Technology has expanded from 700 to 1 100 student spaces. When the expansion programme is completed the institute will have capacity for 2 700 students, enabling it to meet the growing demand for tertiary education generated by rising educational attainment and the trend towards longer periods of study.

Early work on the site provided staff offices and classrooms in an extra storey above the north block. The south block has seen a major extension of existing buildings and new facilities: these include a new library, computer and language suites, four auditoria, a restaurant and cafeteria, reception and administration offices.

The new building is connected to the existing facilities by a top-lit concourse which runs the entire length of the block. It acts as a circulation spine and a place for social interaction, with all student services arranged along its length.

The new building utilises the contours of the site; the stepped auditoria in the new lecture theatres follow the falling ground, a semi-enclosed court space delineated by the new library and computer laboratories is sheltered from the wind by the existing woodland setting.

The extensions allow the institute to respond to new teaching and learning styles. In the library, the reading room is lit from the perimeter windows and a large rooflight above a central well. Built on two levels, it is designed as a flexible space; the floors are zoned to provide a range of spaces from quiet individual reading spaces to group work areas based around computer workstations and multimedia areas.

1

2

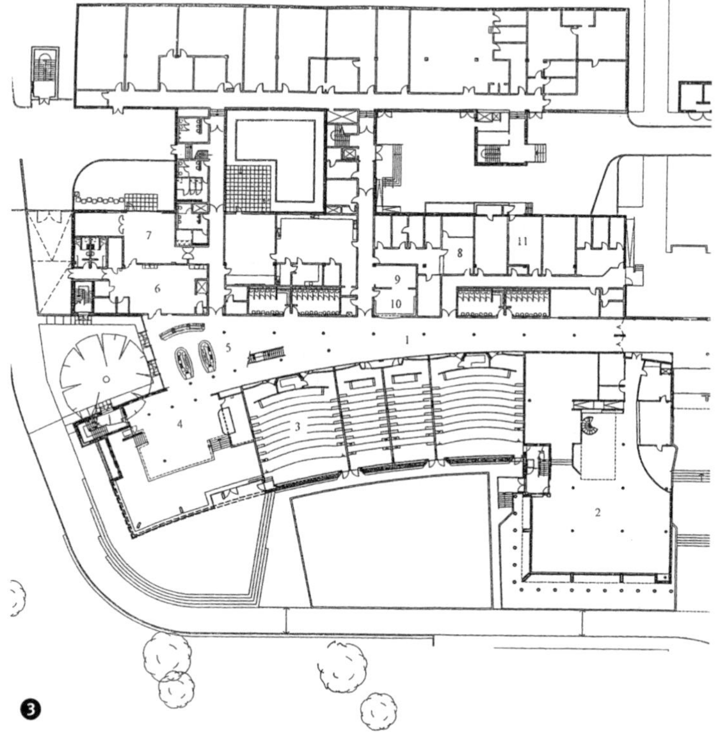

3

Computer suites situated above the lecture theatres have roofs that slope upwards to increase the volume of the space and provide a buffer to the heat output from the computer banks. Elsewhere energy saving and sustainability is a priority as the existing building skin has poor thermal, acoustic and comfort characteristics, however this too is in the process of being upgraded to current standards.

Building against one entire wall of the college has helped inexpensively resolve this issue. The fabric of the building itself provides thermal mass to help reduce temperature fluctuations in all seasons. Materials are chosen on the basis of the renewability of resources, embodied energy, life span, maintenance costs and the potential for recycling.

Photographs courtesy of Christopher Hill Photographic

① *The new extension with the library building in the foreground.*

② *One of the four tiered lecture theatres.*

③ *The ground floor plan.*

④ *The new concourse space.*

⑤ *Food servery at the west end of the concourse.*

⑥ *The new library/reading room.*

ARCHITECT
Architectenbureau A.A. Bos en Partners bv

TYPE OF SCHOOL
Tertiary education

NO. OF STUDENTS
850

AGE RANGE
17 to 25 years

TYPE OF PROJECT
New building

YEAR OF COMPLETION
1996

CLIENT
Stichting Sg.op Reformatorische Grondslag te Gouda

Situated on one of the main roads in Gouda, this new teacher training establishment comprises two wings set at right angles, hinged by a curved building. This element, a 90° sector, contains the main entrance area, the assembly hall, three lecture halls and a large library. It is the public face of the college, a contrast with the "closed" teaching areas in the two wings.

De Driestar College promotes a number of new concepts in teaching, such as teaching as an art, in order to integrate theory and school practice more fully, and achieve greater coherence in the curriculum. Architects AA Bos and Partners have produced a building designed to facilitate the teaching of these new methods.

Structurally, the outer walls, the stairwells and the block containing the toilets and lift form the fixed elements. The rest of the building is divided using modular walls, which allow changes to be made in response to future demands for space. In line with the educational philosophy of the college, a school workshop has been constructed, an interdisciplinary space that can be adapted for different forms of use.

Rather than having long, uniform corridors in the wings, hallways have been widened at points of access to the teaching areas. In effect, the students have to walk from square to square, which encourages communication between students and between students and tutors.

There is an extensive multimedia section in the library and a large area for individual study. There are more than 130 computers in the college. These workstations can be found in the library or teaching workshops. Students are able to use them for their own study or to carry out practical assignments such as developing computer courses and games. In addition, a few classrooms are fully equipped with modern information and communication technology. The college facilities are also available to people from outside the school.

① The assembly hall, situated under lecture halls at the glass-fronted hinge of the college.

② and ③ The library has multimedia resources and student workstations.

④ Linking the two wings, the curved block housing the assembly hall and lecture hall is the public face of the college.

⑤ First floor plan; modular partition walls allow the space to be rearranged to suit a variety of uses.

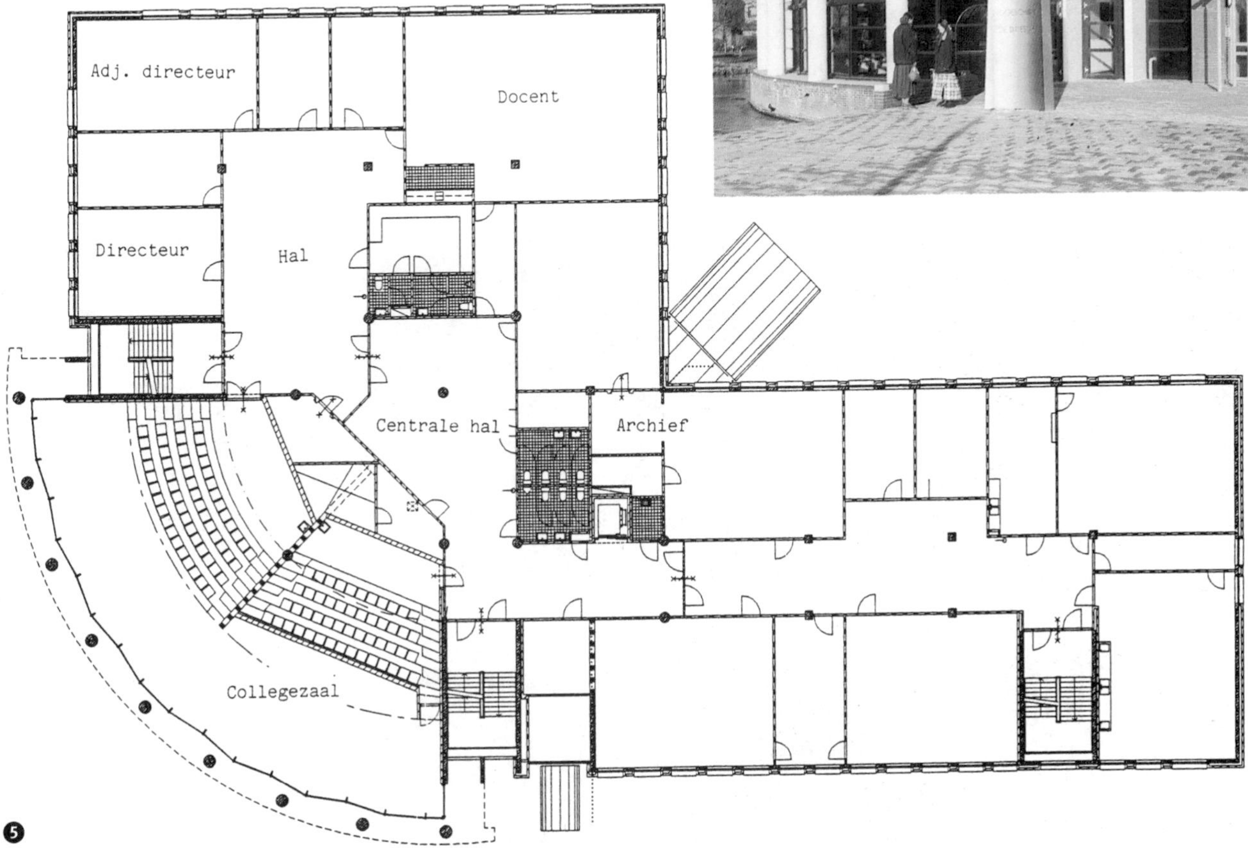

ARCHITECT
Yunken Freeman Architects

TYPE OF SCHOOL
Tertiary education

NO. OF STUDENTS
16 000+

AGE RANGE
16+ years

TYPE OF PROJECT
New building

YEAR OF COMPLETION
2000 continuing

CLIENT
La Trobe University

La Trobe University Bundoora Campus was designed from the outset for growth. Since its foundation, the university has grown rapidly both in terms of students and the number of courses it offers. In 1967, the first enrolment at the university was a mere 552; today, there are more than 16 000 students. But this expansion has been achieved efficiently and harmoniously, creating one of the most attractive parkland campuses in Australia.

Set in a basin site, the increasing student population has been accommodated by both vertical and horizontal expansion. By exemplary land use, the whole campus retains a human scale. There are enclosed links between the buildings, and the site is organised so that no academic building is more than five minutes from the centre of the university complex.

The library, which serves all five faculties and the Institute for Education, is at the centre of the academic complex. It faces a courtyard, which is the hub of the university, a place where students and staff can socialise. The major lecture theatres and the central administrative and commercial functions are also situated here. From this hub, walkways radiate to pass all the seminar rooms and individual buildings.

Buildings are linked by an underground tunnel system, providing an efficient and cost-effective distribution of building and engineering services, and allowing wiring for new technology to be installed with relative ease.

The low-lying campus is prone to flooding and so a flood disaster plan was incorporated into the master plan. The campus is dotted with lakes, and weirs control the water flow. These protect the site from flooding and are an attractive feature in the landscape. Cars are largely excluded from the centre of the campus, and the peripheral car parks are linked to the centre of the campus by a second-level concourse system for safety and personal security.

1

① *The campus from the air; despite the 20-fold increase in students over some forty years, the university environment remains compact yet pleasant.*

② *Covered open walkways radiating out from the central hub link all university facilities and buildings.*

③ *Within the campus, there are many open spaces for students and staff to meet and relax.*

④ *The site plan; the lakes running through the campus are an important element of the water management plan in an area prone to flooding.*

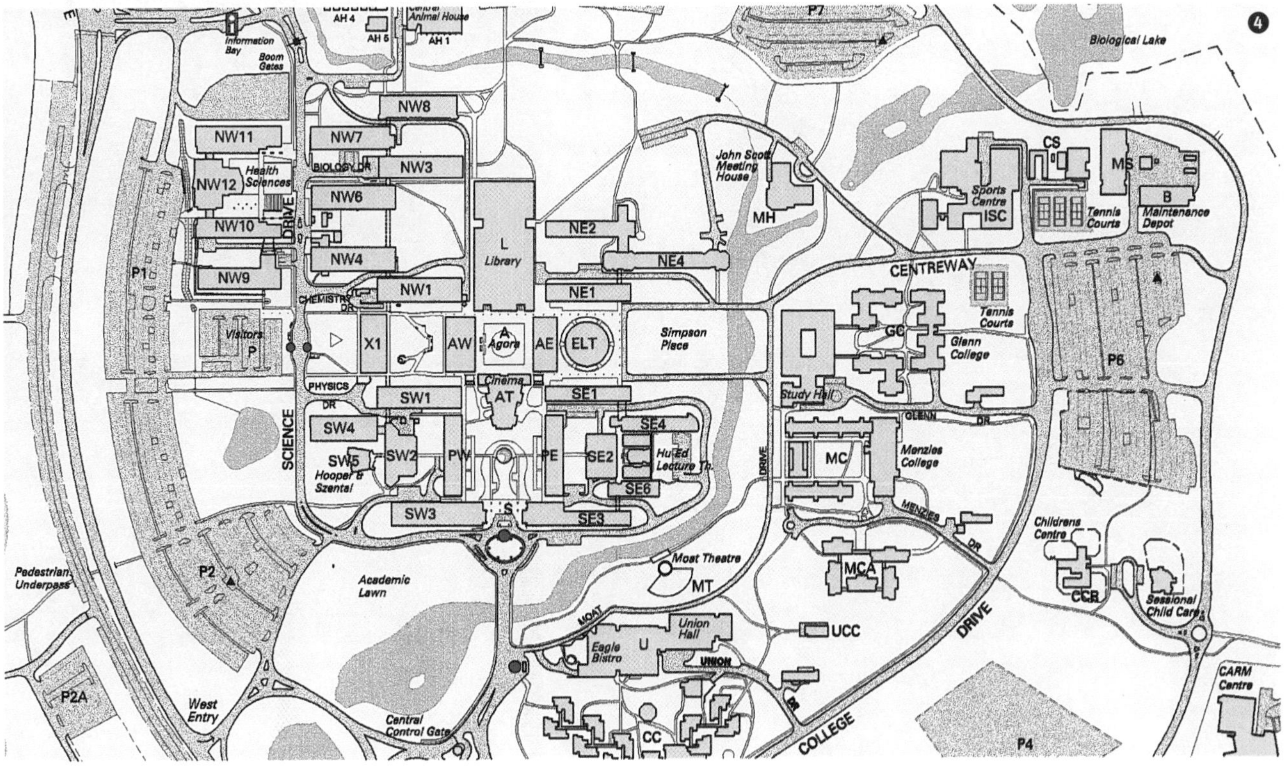

PEB

Chapter four

Strategies for Managing the Educational Infrastructure

Excellence in educational facilities lies not only in the quality of conception and construction, but also in the quality of management. Facility management covers a number of related aspects, and PEB has focused its attention on four in the past five years: maintenance, the utilisation of space, financing, and health and safety.

Good maintenance practice aims to analyse the current condition and suitability of educational facilities, to better understand the whole of life costs of educational assets and to make them more appropriate for current and emerging educational needs.

The inefficient use of space leads to unnecessary recurrent expenditure, to apparent overcrowding of some spaces and underuse of others and to demand for additional buildings. These issues also impact on large school assets. The move to implement lifelong learning and the widespread adoption of information technology will lead to changes in the delivery of educational programmes and the facilities required by institutions.

Capital and recurrent expenditure on educational facilities represents a significant proportion of public expenditure in all OECD countries. In many countries, capital allocations for schools are still related primarily to actual or forecast pupil numbers and do not reflect internal migration, educational or social need, or changing attitudes to lifelong learning.

The health, safety and security of the users of educational facilities are of paramount concern to designers and managers. Staff and students need, so far as is possible, to be safe from natural disaster, as well as from the accidental or deliberate acts of man. Areas of concern include fire prevention, earthquake and disaster management, the quality of the indoor environment, traffic management, controlling hazardous substances, and personal and material security.

The schools and other institutions featured in this chapter demonstrate how innovative approaches can be made to tackling many of these difficult issues.

ARCHITECT
Gudmundur Gunnarsson and Sveinn Ivarsson

TYPE OF SCHOOL
Primary and lower secondary education

NO. OF STUDENTS
450

AGE RANGE
6 to 16 years

TYPE OF PROJECT
New building

YEAR OF COMPLETION
1995

CLIENT
Reykjavik City Council

Built in stages over five years, the completion of Húsaskóli school in a suburb of the capital has finally enabled pupils to move out of the temporary classrooms first erected in 1991. It is perhaps fitting that the materials used for the new building express solidity and permanence; the exterior is built of galvanised steel, with steel and mahogany used for the classrooms and other interior facilities.

Flexibility in the use of space has been one of the prime concerns of the architects. The entrance and seminar hall have been designed for multi-functionality, removing the necessity to build several potentially under-used dedicated spaces. Directly accessible from the exterior, the seminar hall can be reached without causing a disturbance to teachers and pupils. The hall can therefore be used for extra-curricular activities during the school day, to the benefit of the wider community.

Distributed over two floors, the classrooms have been grouped according to purpose. One wing is specifically designed to facilitate small group work; in another, a common space is shared by the younger members of the school community. Communal facilities, such as the library, assembly hall and pupil recreational area, are clustered together in a third section of the building.

This coherence in spatial organisation is reflected in the overall architectural design of the site, which brings together under one roof what had previously been a scattered settlement of temporary buildings. It allows the school to meet educational demand – pupil numbers have increased four-fold in less than ten years – in a modern permanent facility.

1

2

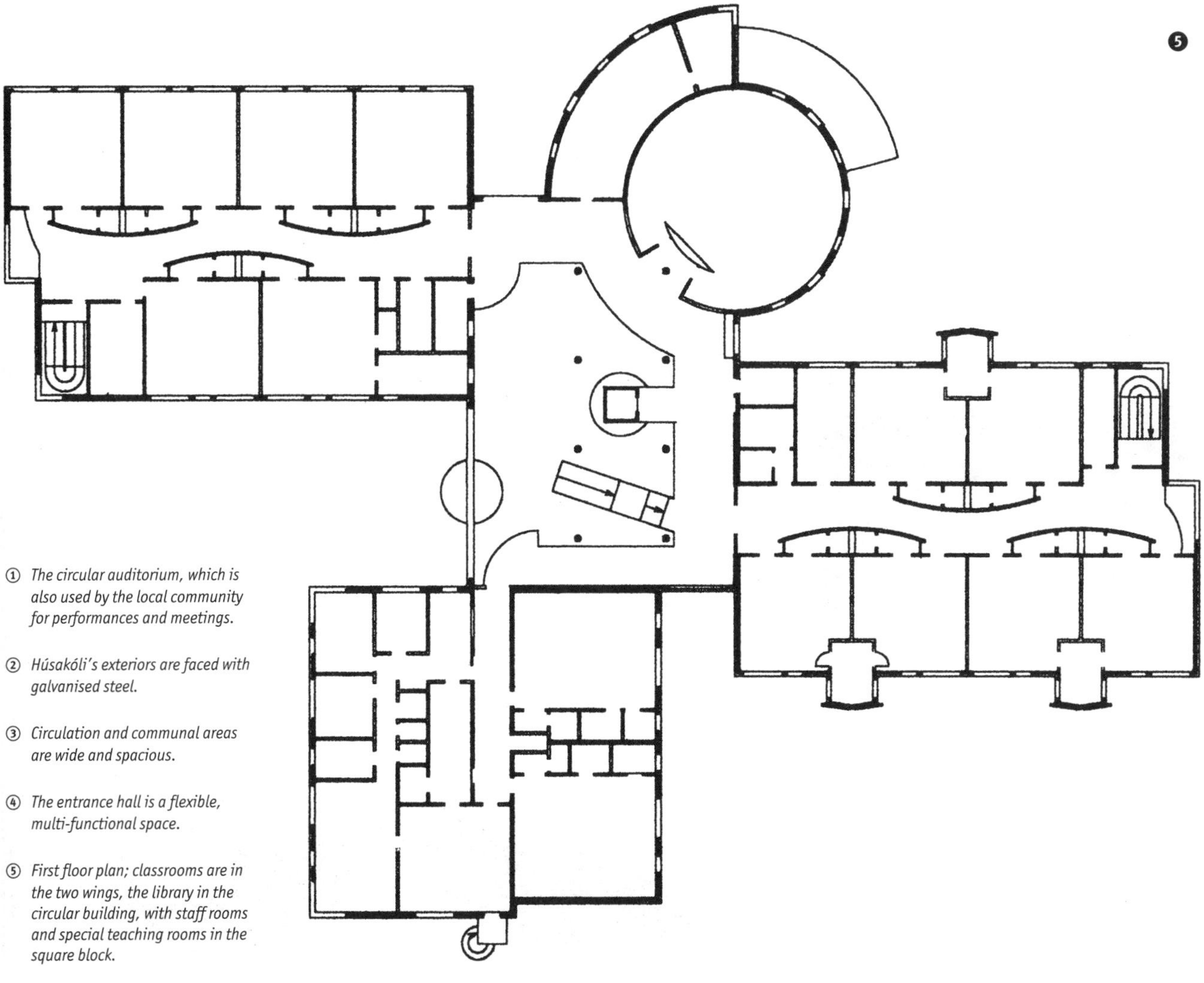

① *The circular auditorium, which is also used by the local community for performances and meetings.*

② *Húsakóli's exteriors are faced with galvanised steel.*

③ *Circulation and communal areas are wide and spacious.*

④ *The entrance hall is a flexible, multi-functional space.*

⑤ *First floor plan; classrooms are in the two wings, the library in the circular building, with staff rooms and special teaching rooms in the square block.*

ARCHITECT
Gernot Kulterer

TYPE OF SCHOOL
Secondary education

NO. OF STUDENTS
900

AGE RANGE
10 to 18 years

TYPE OF PROJECT
Extension/renovation

YEAR OF COMPLETION
1999

CLIENT
Bundesministerium für wirtschaftliche Angelegenheiten

The Allgemeinbildende Höhere Schule in Klagenfurt-Viktring, based within the walls of the twelfth century Viktring monastery, prides itself on being the most beautiful school in Austria. The school's extension and renovation programme has endeavoured to conserve the historic structure while giving pupils access to the latest teaching and learning technologies.

The programme represents the culmination of a long campaign to save a stunning historical monument, which has at various times served as a monastery, a castle and a factory. After the principal offered to take over the building in 1977 to teach children who are exceptionally gifted in music or art, architects worked on a functional and structural guideline which would blend old and new architectural styles.

The latest phase of the renovation programme has extended the school's facilities. Adjoining the baroque church and constructed from wood and steel, the new school library is a distinctive addition to the predominantly stone façade of the monastery. On the upper floor of the north-western wing, new classrooms have been erected using clear glazing, which permits an uninterrupted view of the surrounding medieval fortified wall and its baroque roof truss. Inside the old building, spaces have been modified to make them suitable for exhibitions and public performances.

As a centre of international excellence, the school has benefited greatly from the beauty and atmosphere of the old monastery. Students from as far away as Japan and Iceland now come every summer for classes and concerts. Community feeling is fostered by a setting steeped in tradition. This is a great advantage in a non-urban area, but has also proved crucial in a specialist school dedicated to tapping the creative energies of its pupils.

1

2

❸

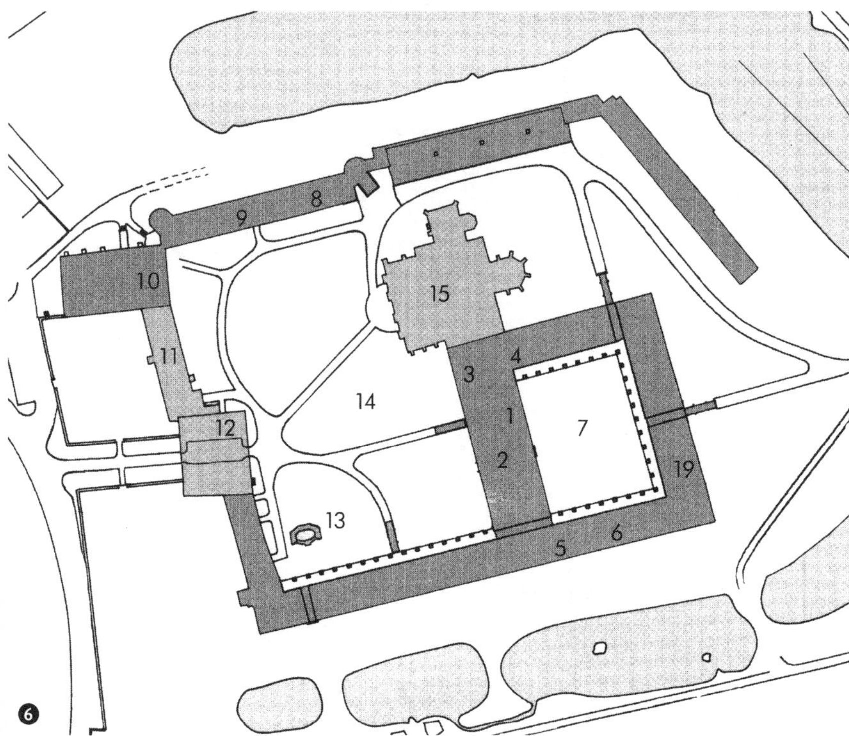

❻

① *Internal rooms have been adapted to create workshops as well as spaces for exhibitions and performances.*

② *The historical setting attracts and inspires music students from around the world.*

③ *The buildings have been imaginatively restored, interweaving modern and historic architectural elements.*

④ *New classrooms and workshops have been created in the upper floor of the monastery, permitting views across the grounds.*

⑤ *Using glass and steel elements, a new library has been incorporated into the main monastery building.*

⑥ *The site plan.*

ARCHITECT
Francisco da Silva Dias

TYPE OF SCHOOL
Vocational education and training

NO. OF STUDENTS
500

AGE RANGE
15 to 22 years

TYPE OF PROJECT
New building

YEAR OF COMPLETION
1992

CLIENT
Escola Profissional da Região Alentejo (EPRAL)

Specialising in vocational education, Epral is a new college. Students have access to the most up-to-date equipment, ensuring that their education takes into account changes in technology and the organisation of the work environment.

Learning zones are organised in such a way so as to accommodate working with equipment on an individual basis or in small groups. This enables the college to deliver the scientific and practical components of courses efficiently. There are laboratories for photographic studies, chemistry and physics, food science, multimedia, electronics, graphic arts and cartography. There is also a training kitchen area where food is produced by catering students.

The resource centre, or mediateca, has several functions: it is a library, holding a growing collection of magazines and journals, interactive computer discs and CD-ROMs, a language and audiovisual laboratory, and a place where Internet research can be conducted.

The school's auditorium can hold around 50 people. It is used for ceremonial occasions, conferences, lectures and seminars, which can be transmitted to the entire school via an internal audiovisual network.

Epral has good links with industry. Through the Fundação Alentejo (the Alentejo Foundation), young graduates who are intending to form their own

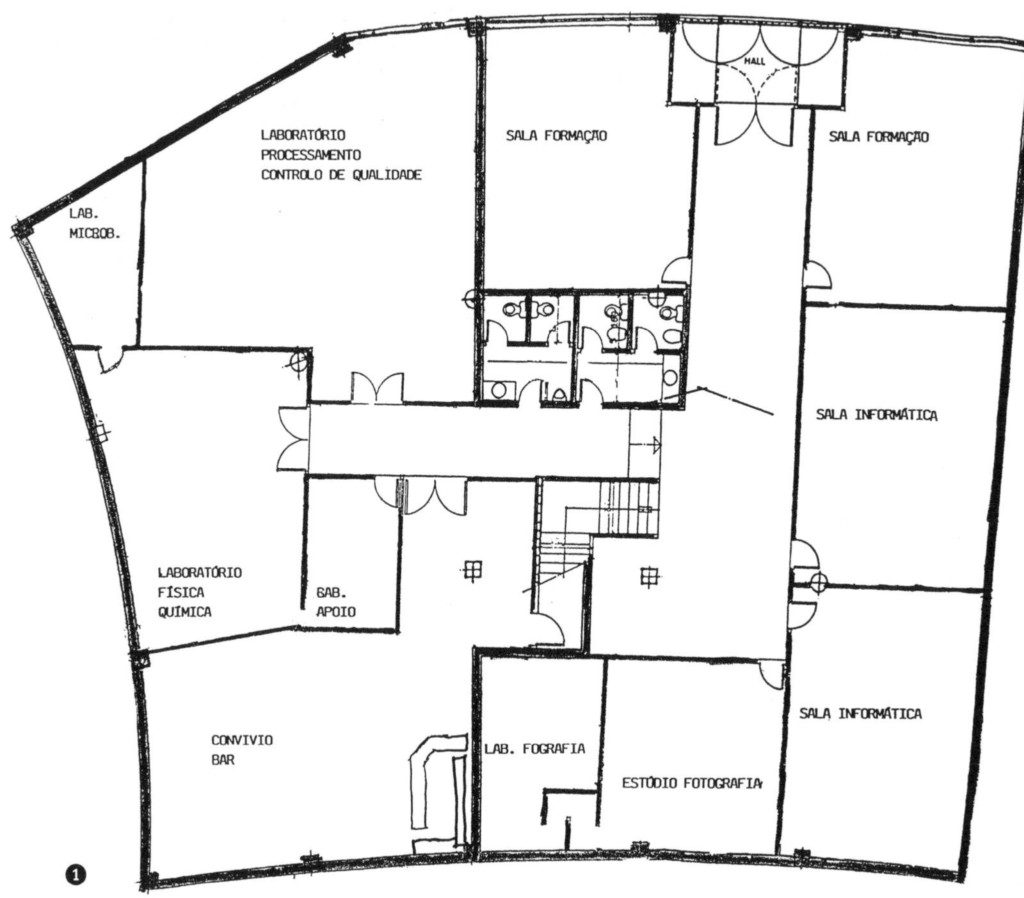

1

companies are able to use Epral's facilities and technical and administrative services free of charge for six months. In addition, an office of continuing education organises ongoing vocational training within the context of national programmes or community initiatives. This is designed to help improve skills and facilitate technological specialisation, and to provide vocational training for the working population.

① *Ground floor plan of one wing of the Epral complex, housing teaching rooms and laboratories.*

② *The school is used day and night, including weekends, to maximise use of the facilities.*

③ *The main auditorium from which lectures can be broadcast over the college's audiovisual network.*

④ *Epral has a fully equipped television and radio studio.*

⑤ *The college library, with computer workstations in the foreground.*

ARCHITECT
José Miguel Regueiras

TYPE OF SCHOOL
Secondary education

NO. OF STUDENTS
500

AGE RANGE
10 to 16 years

TYPE OF PROJECT
New building

YEAR OF COMPLETION
1997

CLIENT
Ministério da Educação

Situated on the banks of the Douro river in the historic centre of Porto, Miragaia High School is in an educational priority area. Economic and social resources are particularly low and there is a high level of illiteracy.

The school has been carefully planned within its compact urban site to maximise the use of available space and resources. All facilities – classrooms, special teaching rooms, libraries, a canteen, sports facilities and recreational and other common areas – are designed to be used by the whole of the school. These facilities are also open to parents, community bodies and sports clubs. To improve space utilisation, the school is developing a flexible curriculum management programme, which allows the syllabus to be integrated with the educational needs of the school community. It also opens up the facilities outside school hours, allowing the building to be used in the evenings and at weekends.

Information and communication technology is an integral part of the school. Pupils are encouraged to use this technology in accessing information and producing work. Facilities include a radio studio for internal broadcasting, a computer science room where a school newspaper is produced, a library and resource centre with Internet access, photo and video libraries, and a room for playing audio and video materials.

The school has helped transform the local environment. The site was formerly derelict, and the energy-efficient buildings are designed both to introduce new levels of quality of construction into the area and to respect the local surroundings. Horto das Virtudes, one of the parks which surround the school, has been restored to its former state after having lain abandoned for 60 years. This not only benefits the local community but also the school, as the park is used by pupils for biology fieldwork and environmental studies.

1

2

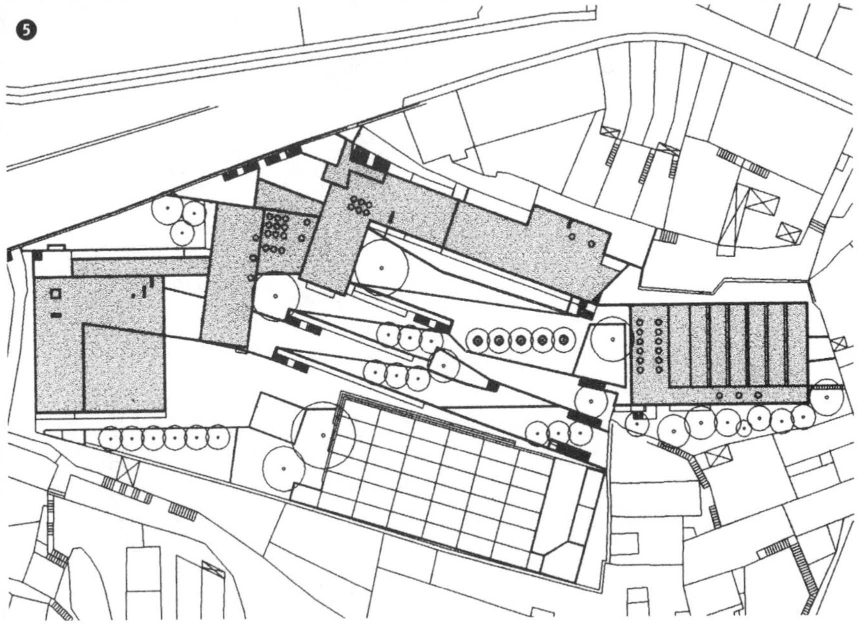

① *One of the corridors within the long linear plan.*

② *Situated on the steep banks of the Douro, the school buildings have been designed to make the most use of the compact urban site.*

③ *Students in the school cafeteria.*

④ *View from a corridor across the rooftops of old Porto.*

⑤ *Site plan; the buildings are arranged to suit the contours of the site.*

ARCHITECT
Architekten Nehrer + Medek und Partner

TYPE OF SCHOOL
Vocational education and training, adult education

NO. OF STUDENTS
1700

AGE RANGE
14 to 19 years

TYPE OF PROJECT
Extension/renovation

YEAR OF COMPLETION
1998

CLIENT
Bundesimmobilien-gesellschaft

Formerly situated in the city centre, this vocational and technical college has been forced to relocate to the outskirts of the city due to lack of space to meet demand. It is now housed in a former tobacco works at Ottakring, now an area of urban regeneration. A classified historical monument, it is owned by the Federal Real Estate Company, which has restored the building, adding a sympathetic new extension, and leased the facility to the college.

The old tobacco works is used by the college for workshops, laboratories and special classrooms, as the height of the ceilings allows room for engineering equipment. The classrooms and art rooms are in the new building. There is also room for a cafeteria and a gymnasium which were not on the original site.

Dividing partitions in the old factory hall have large windows to preserve the spatial characteristics of the original construction. The extension receives natural daylight through a continuous series of windows on the outside and corridor walls and large skylights. Classrooms are bright, provided with external shades to lessen the intensity of the sunlight if necessary.

The college's electronic data processing infrastructure has been extended since the move and 170 new workstations have been added to the 90 that have been created with older equipment. Other modern facilities have been added, including a photovoltaic power supply which is used for research and to teach students about alternative power sources as well as for supplying energy.

An active partnership has been established between industry and the college, providing financial support for the purchasing and maintenance of technical equipment. Around 50 collaborative projects with industry and commerce are carried out yearly.

Students have responded positively to the new environment and facilities. Motivation has increased and acts of vandalism have decreased since the move.

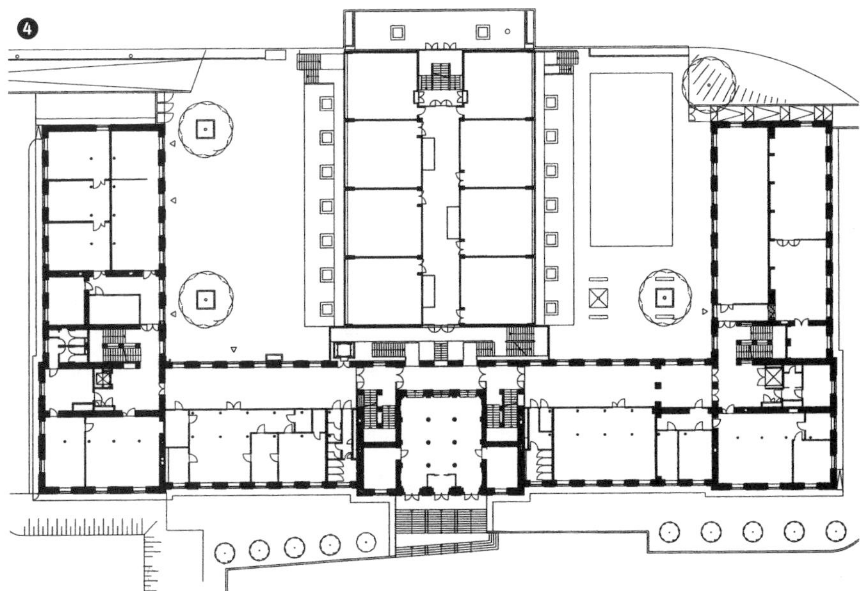

① *More than 250 computer workstations are provided in the college's new premises at Ottakring.*

② *The compact modern extension provides a base for the classrooms, with a gymnasium in the basement.*

③ *The linking corridor and stairs between the new extension and the tobacco works; large windows and skylights provide ample natural light.*

④ *The ground floor plan; the new extension (top centre) is parallel to the two wings of the old tobacco works, set perpendicular to the main building.*

⑤ *With its impressive brick façade, the former Austria Tabakwerke building houses the college's reception area, laboratories and technical workshops.*

ARCHITECT
Jean-Marc Coursol

TYPE OF SCHOOL
Vocational education and training

NO. OF STUDENTS
500

AGE RANGE
20 to 50 years

TYPE OF PROJECT
Extension and renovation

YEAR OF COMPLETION
1997

CLIENT
Commission scolaire de la Rivière-du-Nord

Designated by the Quebec Ministry of Education as one of the two public schools in the province to award a diploma in vocational study for lorry driving, the Saint-Jérôme training centre moved into its new premises in 1997. Having operated in a cramped environment over many years, the move has enabled the centre to accommodate the latest technology and use available space more efficiently. The move has been welcomed by staff, trainee lorry drivers and employers alike.

With its emphasis on continuous professional development, the centre has sought to create a space which accurately reflects the realities of working life in the transport industry. The architectural style of construction, with its facing of stone and metallic cladding, borrows from styles common in industrial buildings. By extending the existing buildings, the maintenance and washing bays have been brought together and additional space is available to practice reversing and transfer of merchandise. Driving practice is supervised from a look-out, from where all the road circuits can be seen.

Through renovating existing buildings and adding extensions, the designers have improved the adaptability of the site to teaching and training functions. Laboratories and demonstration areas have been grouped near the classrooms, and sites for practical teaching are located near the parking lots and road circuits. This layout reflects the content of the course, which is largely practical but includes a substantial element of theory.

Completed within budget, the renovation programme has increased the capacity of

1

2

the training centre. The teaching areas have been improved and the movement of traffic on site is safer for pedestrians. Staff have noted an immediate beneficial impact on the quality of their working environment as well as their teaching practice: air quality, sound proofing, lighting and space management have all been enhanced. The completed project has managed to strike a harmonious balance between architectural aesthetics and pedagogical functionality.

① *Interiors have a practical, business-like feel; reception and welcome area.*

② *View from the air; the site has plenty of space for parking and practising driving manoeuvres.*

③ *Functional and workmanlike; the centre's cafeteria.*

④ *Large garages provide space for practical workshops and demonstrations.*

⑤ *Floor plan; the extensions at each end of the building provide extensive workshop space.*

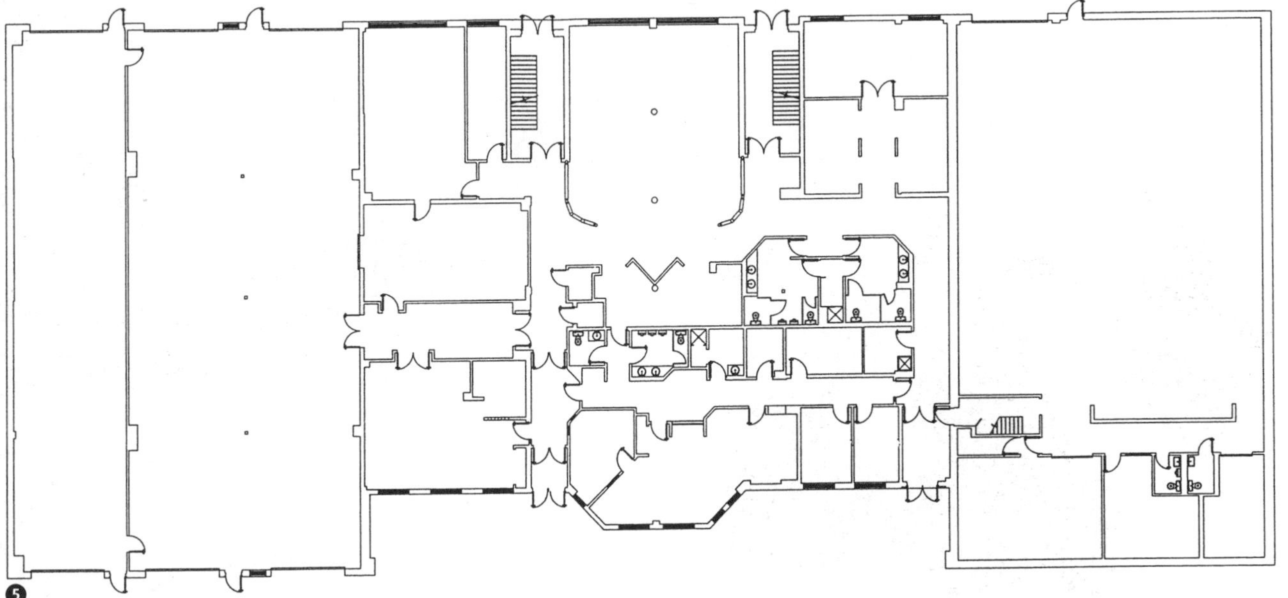

ARCHITECT
C.A.P.F.C.E.

TYPE OF SCHOOL
Primary education

NO. OF STUDENTS
220

AGE RANGE
6 to 12 years

TYPE OF PROJECT
Renovation

YEAR OF COMPLETION
1999

CLIENT
Secretary of Education

Pupils at Francisco Beltrán Otero School mostly come from low income backgrounds and it is important that the school facilities are modern, clean, well illuminated and spacious in order to help promote self esteem and a spirit of collaboration amongst the pupils.

Francisco Beltrán Otero School exemplifies the collaborative approach that is necessary for the running of state schools in less affluent areas. Normal wear and tear, and in some cases vandalism, impose a heavy burden on school maintenance. But in the last three years, local communities have helped with school maintenance through voluntary work by teachers and parents on Saturdays.

Using materials provided by the Department of Education, they help with activities such as window pane replacement, repainting, repair of furniture and the cleaning and repair of sanitary facilities. As a result of this collaborative programme, the standard of facilities has increased, parents have shown commitment to the school – indeed some parents have attended lectures on parenting skills and in some cases adult literacy – and ultimately the children have benefited.

Financial assistance is also provided by Comparte, the Department of Education's voluntary arm. At the moment it procures investment from the private sector bodies that provide maintenance material or cash for school maintenance through its School Adoption scheme. Representatives have attended the World Bank's Development Market Place in search of more funding to develop the school's facilities.

The school itself has four main classroom blocks, a forum for cultural activities, a plaza for outdoor activities – with an area covered with a metallic roof to give some protection from the sun – and areas for sports. A fifth multipurpose building is due to be added soon.

1

2

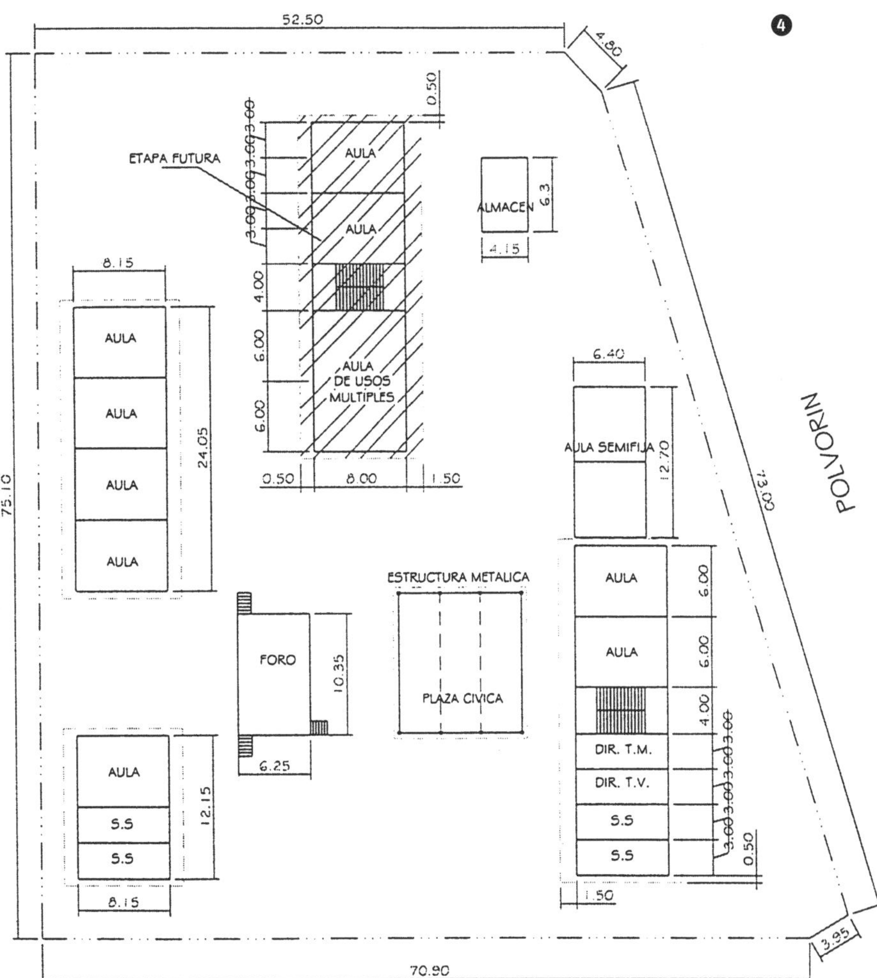

① *Pupils watching television in one of the classrooms.*

② *The school buildings are arranged around a plaza, which is used for play and community activities.*

③ *There is room on the site to build additional school facilities.*

④ *The site plan.*

⑤ *An open covered space provides children with some protection against the sun at play times.*

⑥ *Parents have played a full part in the school's renovation programme, helping to replace and repair windows and furniture and to redecorate classrooms.*

ARCHITECT
Orcan Gündüz

TYPE OF SCHOOL
Pre-school, primary education, lower secondary education

NO. OF STUDENTS
432 (total capacity)

AGE RANGE
5 to 13 years

TYPE OF PROJECT
New building

YEAR OF COMPLETION
1999

CLIENT
Dokuz Eylul University Foundation

Dokuz Eylul University Foundation 75th Year Primary and Secondary School is a private school. It has been developed by Dokuz Eylul University as a contribution to Turkey's national education policy of integrating primary and secondary (middle) schools; the idea being to promote interaction between different age groups. The school is situated on the new university campus on the outskirts of Buca, a town close to Izmir.

The first phase of building has been completed with the university members offering voluntary help throughout the design, implementation, fundraising, introduction and operation of the project. The second phase, which includes the pre-school buildings and multipurpose hall, is due for completion in the summer of 2001.

As a private school in competition with others for fee-paying pupils, it is thought that both its architectural and educational qualities have a role in attracting students. The school is designed as an active learning centre, utilising the educational potential of the university and ideally producing future university students. It comprises educational, administrative and pre-school units as well as recreational areas and sports facilities.

The L-shaped building demonstrates the sequential arrangement of space from public (the main courtyard), semi-public (canopy and corridors), to private (the classrooms). This is a contemporary version of building design that has been implemented in the Aegean area since the Greek and Roman eras, and in traditional Turkish settlements. To encourage social integration, communal spaces are attractive and well lit. Access ramps, an elevator and the toilets have all been designed to accommodate pupils with disabilities.

The building complex is oriented away from the cold north winds and faces south towards the courtyard. The inner court façade is covered by a canopy (portico) which shelters students from rain and the hot summer sun. This environmentally conscious design has saved energy expenditure in its first year.

❷

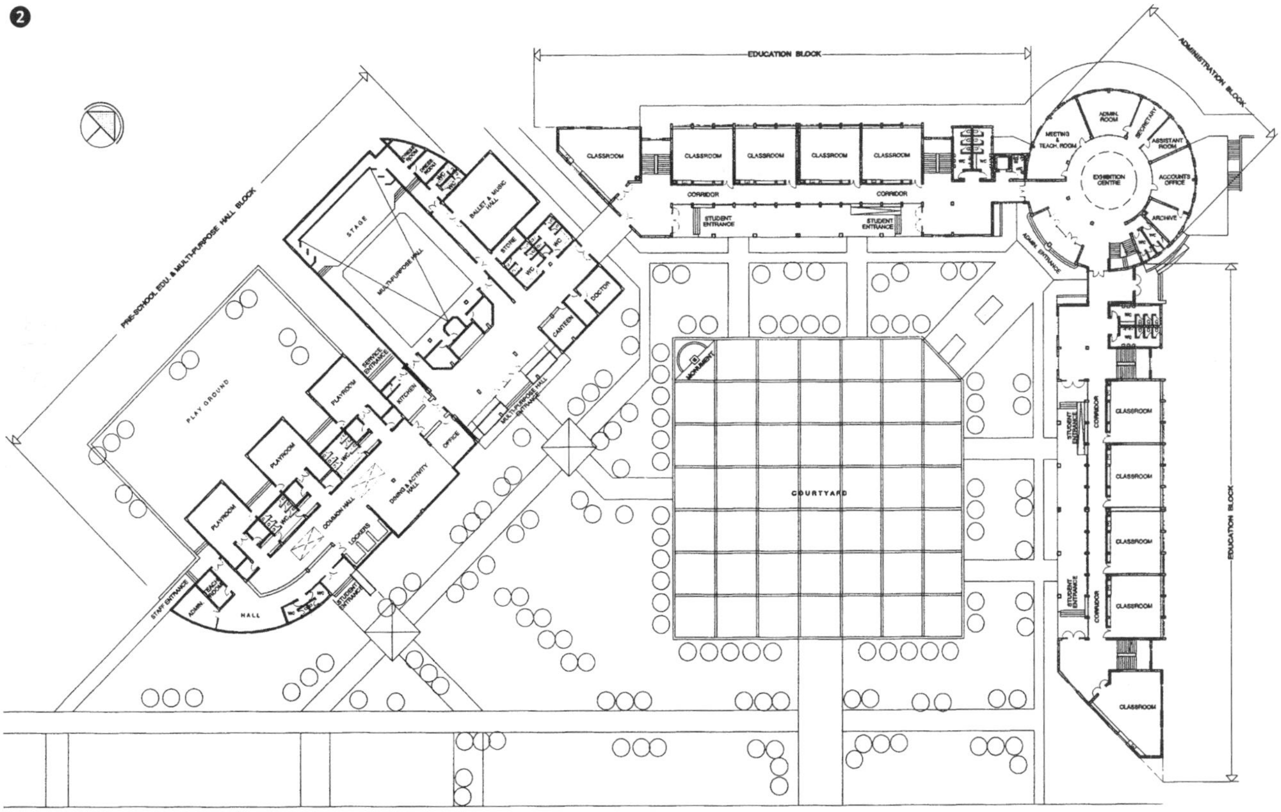

① *View from the courtyard; the school has an L-shaped plan and is oriented to provide a sheltered environment.*

② *The ground floor plan; two education blocks are joined by the circular administration building. The attached blocks house the multipurpose hall, music/drama rooms and the pre-school.*

③ *Staff rooms and offices circle the atrium and exhibition space at the centre of the administrative unit.*

④ *View from the north; the circular building houses offices, staff rooms, the library and the dining hall on the ground floor.*

ARCHITECT
Terence O'Rourke plc

TYPE OF SCHOOL
Secondary education

NO. OF STUDENTS
1060

AGE RANGE
11 to 18 years

TYPE OF PROJECT
New building

YEAR OF COMPLETION
1999

CLIENT
Dorset County Council

Sir John Colfox School is the first secondary school in the UK to be built under the Private Finance Initiative, a government scheme designed to attract private sector investment into public sector capital projects. This financial route has not led to any compromise in the quality of the scheme, a completely new building on the site of a former school.

The head teacher and staff have been involved throughout the design process, which was based on sustainable principles. The new school includes a main hall, general teaching rooms, a library, facilities for people with special needs and specialist teaching accommodation for science, languages, technology, art, drama and music. There are good catering and dining facilities and a sports hall.

The aim of the school is to improve educational standards and attainment levels through the provision of modern facilities and the creation of conducive working environments. Energy efficient heating and appropriate acoustic insulation create spaces with comfortable learning conditions. The functional grouping of rooms and linkage between departments cut down the unnecessary movement of pupils. An internal glazed "street" runs the length of the school and links all the separate buildings. Together with light wells and an atrium, it ensures there is plenty of natural daylight in the school.

A variety of social spaces are provided to create a sense of belonging and ownership. These include an amphitheatre, a cloistered garden, seating within the glazed street, a café, external teaching areas and a pond.

Outside school hours, the school facilities are used by the local community. This was a consideration from the beginning of the project and the community was consulted throughout the different stages of the design.

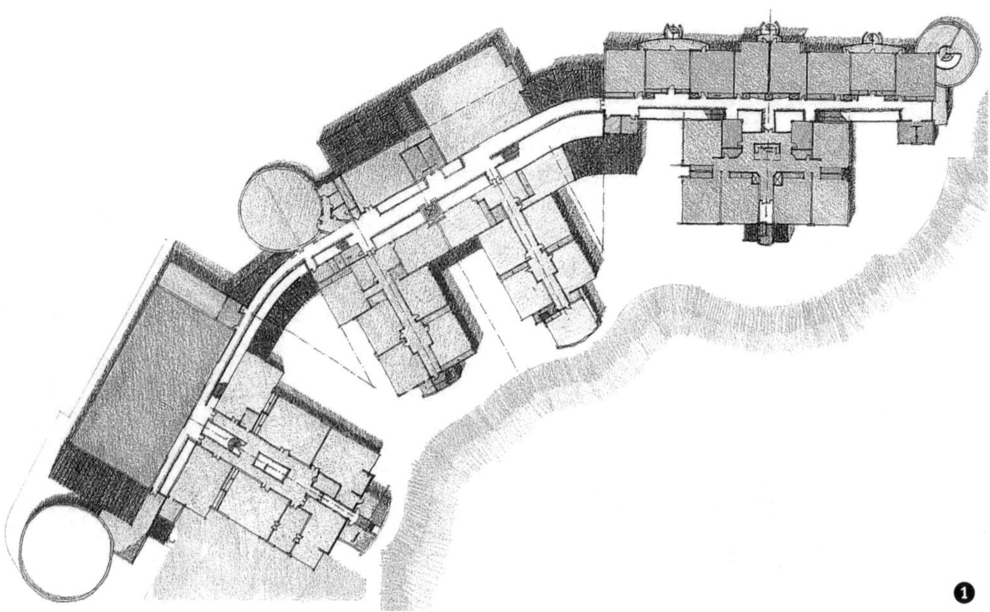

1

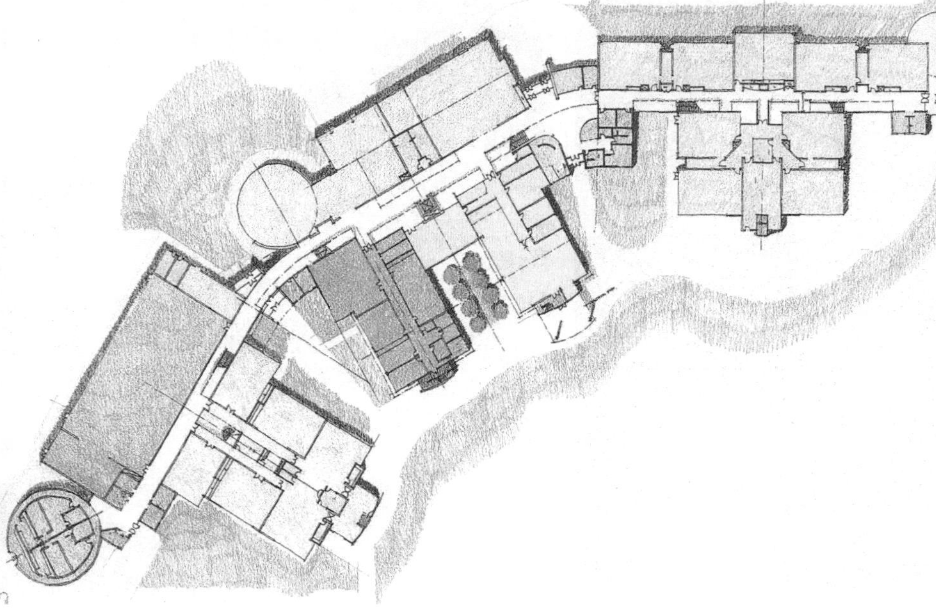

① *First floor plan; teaching areas are organised in departmental groups.*

② *The school backs on to extensive sports grounds.*

③ *Stairwells and corridors are spacious and well lit.*

④ *The two-storey brick buildings are set in attractive grounds.*

⑤ *The circular dining room looks out on the school grounds.*

⑥ *Ground floor plan; an internal street links all elements of the school. The library and information technology centre (yellow) is located in the middle of the complex.*

ARCHITECT
Eugène Moureau

TYPE OF SCHOOL
Tertiary education

NO. OF STUDENTS
1 500

AGE RANGE
18 to 25 years

TYPE OF PROJECT
Renovation

YEAR OF COMPLETION
2000

CLIENT
Institut Supérieur des Beaux-Arts et Institut Supérieur d'Architecture Saint Luc, Liège

The development of this new tertiary education establishment has taken place on the site of a former army barracks; the complex includes an eighteenth century chapter house and a nineteenth century riding school. The project involves the integration of two formerly independent schools, an art school and a school of architecture, which occupied buildings that had become dilapidated and unsuitable to a modern educational approach.

Respecting the integrity and quality of the site's historic heritage, the renovation exhibits a desire for openness in contrast to the assertive austerity of the military architecture. It is hoped that the development will breath new life into this district of Liège.

The first stage of the project consisted of adapting the buildings to their new functions. For example, painting and sculpture workshops have been created by adapting and adding services into a former warehouse and garages. Administrative functions have been housed in historic buildings at the heart of the complex. A second stage of additions and conversions is planned over the next four years.

The scattered aspect of the buildings, together with their disposition in a sort of mini-village, meant that after appropriate architectural intervention, two types of space are offered to students and teachers: private areas for courses, classes and workshops and common spaces, both interior and exterior, for social interaction.

Architectural intervention has been discreet and to some extent neutral, with an absence of colour or decoration. The effect of this has been to free up the buildings to form collective spaces for the exchange of ideas and to encourage students to express themselves.

1

2

The infrastructure has been put in place to support an information network. To enable communication within the school as well as exchanges with the outside, the network provides computer links between principal centres on the site. Telephone lines, computers, projectors and information monitors are connected to a general network with the latest fibre-optic technology.

③

④

❺
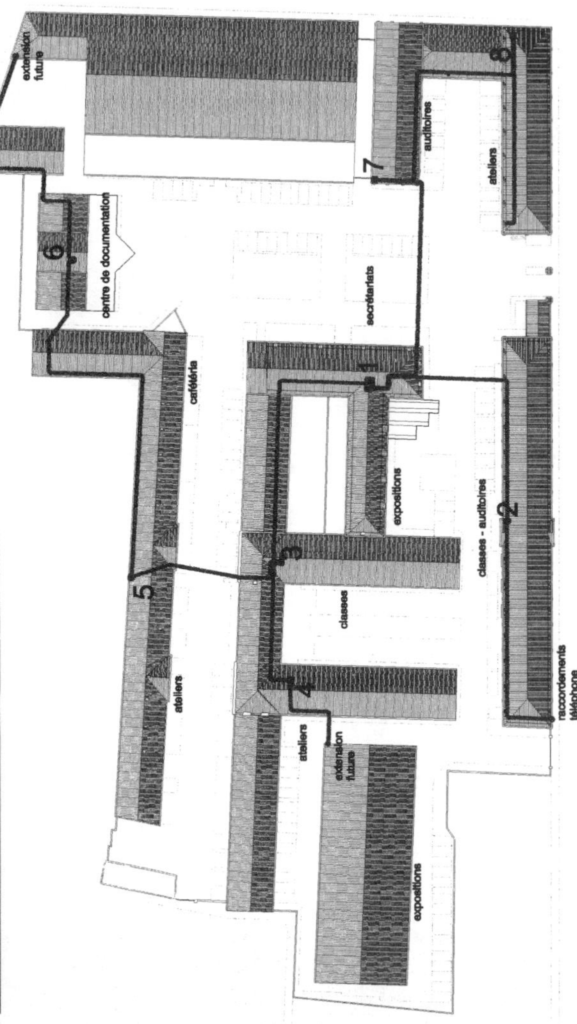

① *Set in a former army barracks, the challenge has been to convert the buildings for educational use while retaining the integrity of the original structures.*

② *Warehouses and garages have been converted into workshops and study areas. Light and openess contrast with the austerity of the former military architecture.*

③ *Internally, the building has been modified to allow large rooms for art and design works and exhibitions.*

④ *Colours and finishes have been kept neutral, encouraging students to express ideas freely.*

⑤ *With its former scattered buildings and street pattern, the campus of the Beaux-Arts and Architecture school in Liège has a village feel. Internal and external common spaces allow for social interaction; an information network provides virtual interaction.*

ARCHITECT
Architekten Nehrer + Medek und Partner

TYPE OF SCHOOL
Secondary education, vocational education and training

NO. OF STUDENTS
1300

AGE RANGE
10 to 19 years

TYPE OF PROJECT
New building

YEAR OF COMPLETION
1997

CLIENT
Bundesimmobilien-gesellschaft (BIG)

Built on a site owned by the Federal Real Estate Company, this new high school and business school in Vienna is managed on private sector lines.

Included in its leasing arrangements with the real estate company is a provision for the maintenance of the building. The upkeep of facilities is therefore financed, and can be planned for, in advance.

The school places particular emphasis on strengthening the links between the classroom and the workplace, to facilitate a more flexible approach to learning and professional development. Training is carried out using real-world examples, in some cases supported by local businesses.

In the school's Centre for Applied Economics, for example, teachers organise activities which simulate all the processes of a real business. Classrooms are furnished in an office style, and students perform roles across a range of functional areas, such as marketing, procurement, sales and personnel. This approach, known as practice enterprises or training firms, is built around genuine team work between students as well as role playing with teachers.

While the practice enterprise is designed to simulate a market economy, the school also encourages students to engage in the real economy by creating junior firms. These involve students – with guidance from expert teachers – trading actual goods or services, using real money.

Equipped with all the latest office and information technologies, the Centre for Applied Economics delivers education in all areas of business. It aims to improve the transparency of qualifications and relevance of training, ensuring that students' skills can be applied as soon as they enter industry.

① *Circular glass-fronted rooms occupy one corner of each of the three wings, providing a space for meetings and other "business" activities.*

② *and* ③ *Glass and steel elements are used to good effect.*

④ *The gymnasium.*

⑤ *The site plan.*

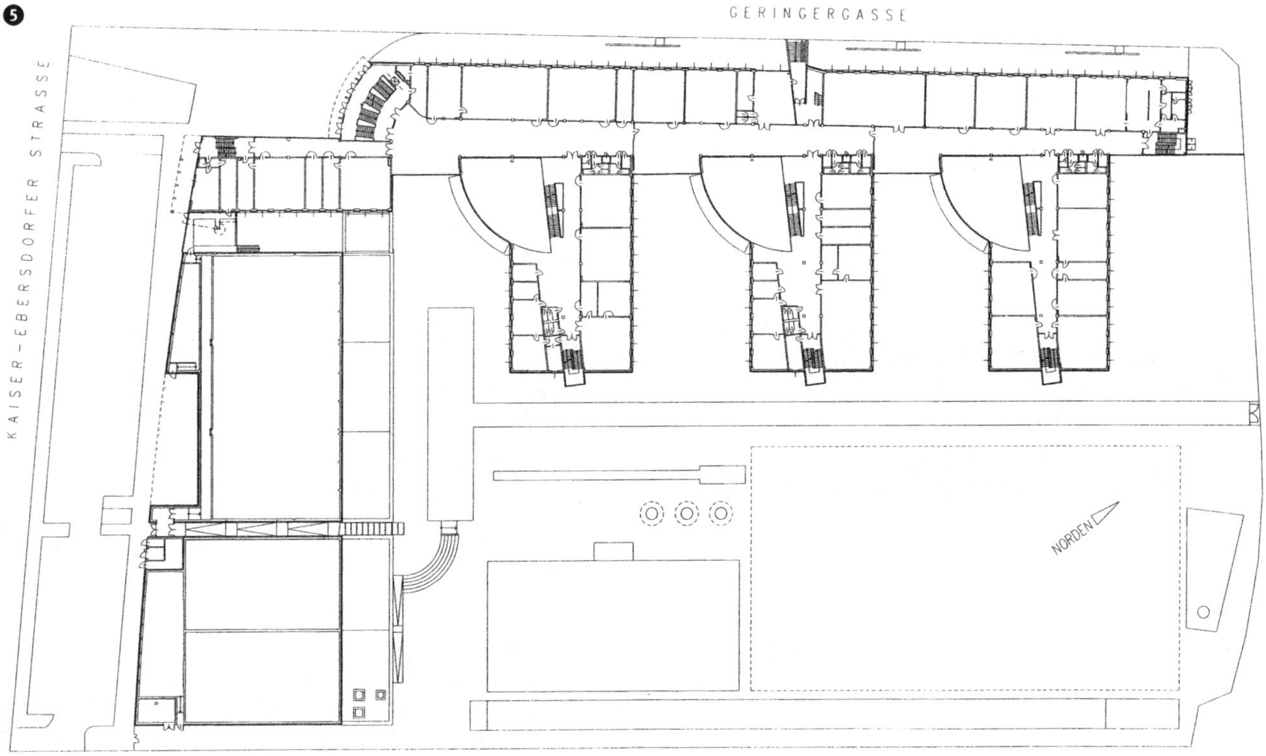

ARCHITECT
Unicorn Consultancy Services (in succession to BRETS)

TYPE OF SCHOOL
Pre-school and primary education

NO. OF STUDENTS
800

AGE RANGE
3 to 11 years

TYPE OF PROJECT
New building

YEAR OF COMPLETION
1999

CLIENT
London Borough of Ealing

The school that the new Willow Tree Primary School replaces had a sprawling, inefficient plan and was becoming increasingly uneconomic to maintain. The floor area of the new school is about half that of the old facility.

Although the school is large, the arrangement of the accommodation enables the pupils to identify with their area and provides an environment conducive to learning. Classrooms are arranged in pairs and in age sequence – nursery, reception infants and juniors. Each pair of classrooms shares a private external quiet play area, a small cloakroom and a toilet. These are situated around a central area containing halls, an atrium, shared resources and service areas.

Information technology is given high priority. The school has a structured cabling network which provides both voice and data connections. This gives direct access to the Internet and to large, fixed, interactive whiteboards in each classroom. Teachers can use the Internet directly with the whole class – in fact it is possible for all 700 students to use the Internet at the same time. This highly visual medium serves to motivate the children, who can see their work on the large or small screen. Team work is strengthened by teachers emailing lesson plans and presentations to all staff members.

Although the school is situated on a sloping site, the building is fully accessible to people with disabilities. Ramps connect the three levels on the ground floor, and a lift gives access to accommodation on the first floor.

The building is particularly well insulated, and all external windows and roof lights are double glazed. The fully integrated

building service installation includes underfloor heating. Building insurance premiums have been reduced by installing a sprinkler system throughout.

For increased safety, several security systems are used, including controlled entry, intruder alarms and closed circuit television.

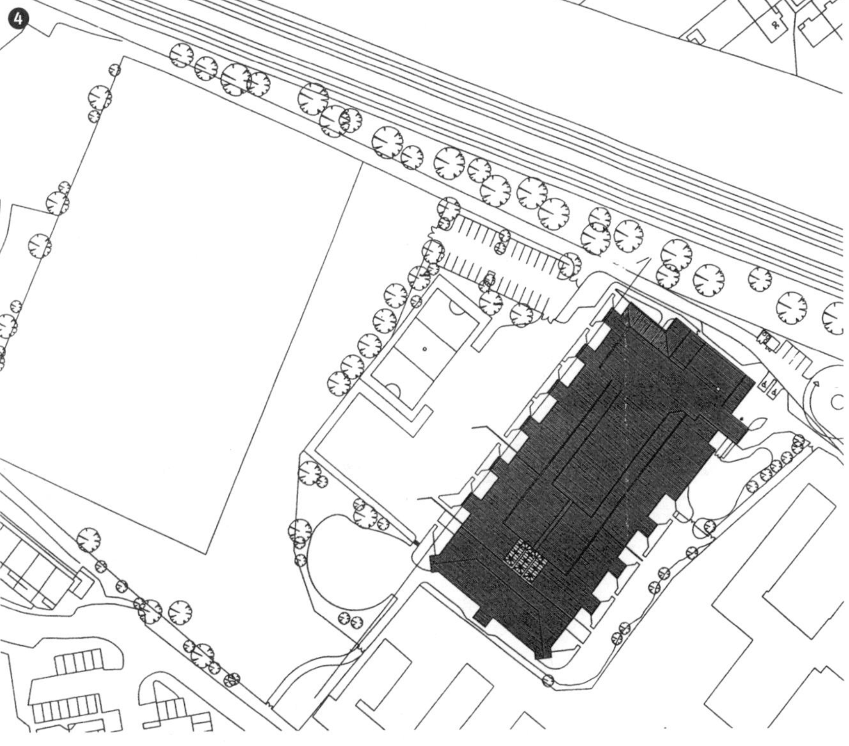

① The school entrance; security is enhanced by controlled entry, intruder alarms and closed circuit television.

② In addition to the main playground, each pair of classrooms has an enclosed private play area.

③ All classes have direct access to the Internet through interactive whiteboards.

④ Site plan; the new school (shaded) is bounded by the underground line, playing fields and the site of the old school which has been demolished.

⑤ The south-west elevation.

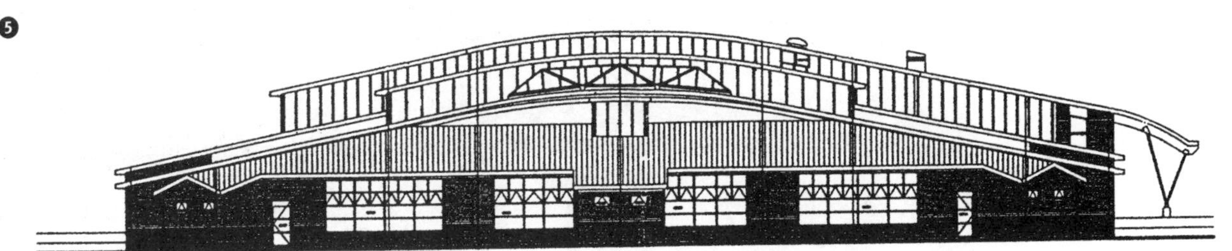

ARCHITECT
Jorge Manuel Farelo Pinto

TYPE OF SCHOOL
Secondary education

NO. OF STUDENTS
1260

AGE RANGE
12 to 18 years

TYPE OF PROJECT
New building

YEAR OF COMPLETION
1986

CLIENT
Ediçor

Situated on one of the mid-Atlantic volcanic islands in the Azores, this school has been designed to take account of the fact that the region experiences tremors and earthquakes without warning. It is therefore constructed to resist them in accordance with regional building standards.

It is divided into two independent blocks – the two-storey school building and the sports complex. The classrooms are mainly situated on the upper floor with easy access to the outside via staircases. At the end of each is an emergency exit door which can easily be opened from the inside. The school is properly equipped to reduce the risk of fire, and regular checks are undertaken by the fire service. Emergency evacuation procedures are tested regularly under the supervision of the Civil Protection Services.

On the ground floor there are science laboratories, computer rooms and an administrative area. There is also a library and a hall, where temporary exhibitions often take place. The lecture theatre has a capacity of 200 and is frequently used by members of the community for meetings and other functions. The cafeteria is also open to people from outside the school on special occasions. The sports facilities are housed in an

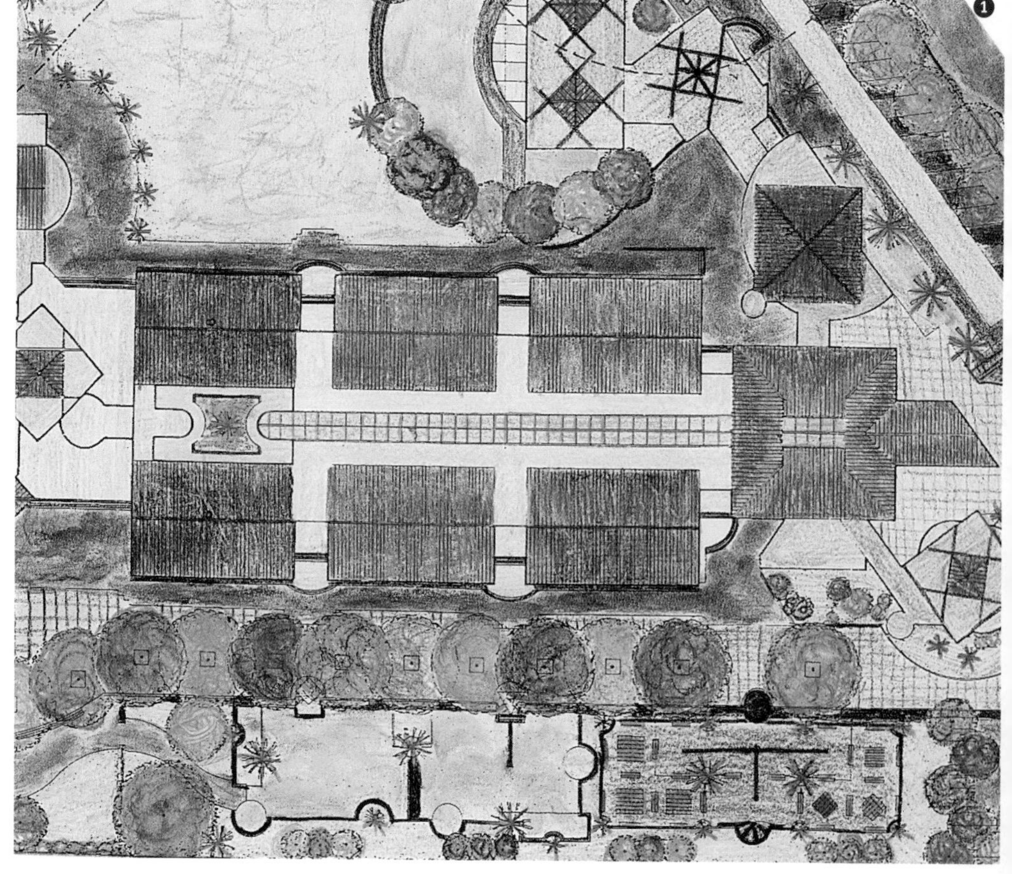

adjoining building. Managed independently, they are open to the public at evenings and weekends.

The grounds are laid out with lawns, trees and benches. A herb and vegetable garden is used for teaching purposes, particularly by pupils who are preparing for careers in agronomy. The school contains a covered interior courtyard with seats and tables where pupils can socialise.

① *Site plan; the school is organised into two blocks. One of them has a central covered courtyard.*

② *The main entrance, which leads to the courtyard and the ground floor laboratories and computer rooms.*

③ *The library, with exhibits devoted to the island's volcanic origin on the table (foreground).*

④ *Students during a physical education lesson in the school gymnasium.*

⑤ *A view down the central internal courtyard which links the separate teaching blocks.*

ARCHITECT
School Building Organisation S.A.

TYPE OF SCHOOL
Upper secondary education

NO. OF STUDENTS
240

AGE RANGE
12 to 15 years

TYPE OF PROJECT
New building

YEAR OF COMPLETION
1999

CLIENT
S.B.O.

Designed to harmonise with the surrounding natural environment, this new school is also built to withstand environmental dangers. Its frame has been constructed to high specifications to take into account the risk of earthquakes. The building is constructed with brick and concrete to minimise fire risk and has external, in addition to two internal, fire escapes.

Situated at the site's high point to take advantage of views, all levels of the school receive natural light, providing both a source of illumination within the buildings and passive solar energy. The school is oriented to maximise this passive energy gain. As the buildings within the complex are linked and compact, insulation is afforded by the mass of the structure of the school itself. Energy is also conserved by insulation of the walls, floors and roof of the building.

All windows are double-glazed. The corridors and all the classrooms have high-level opening lights to ensure a good standard of natural ventilation.

Elements of classical Greek architecture have been incorporated into the design of the buildings. The choice of materials and massing provides an attractive and appropriate scale and the site has been sensitively landscaped: this outdoor environment will improve as the planting matures. An elevator and a ramp have been constructed to cater for people with special needs.

Use of space is economical and the plan form allows for considerable flexibility in practical use. The setting of windows at regular intervals, the structural frame and non-load bearing partitions all allow for long-term adaptability.

4

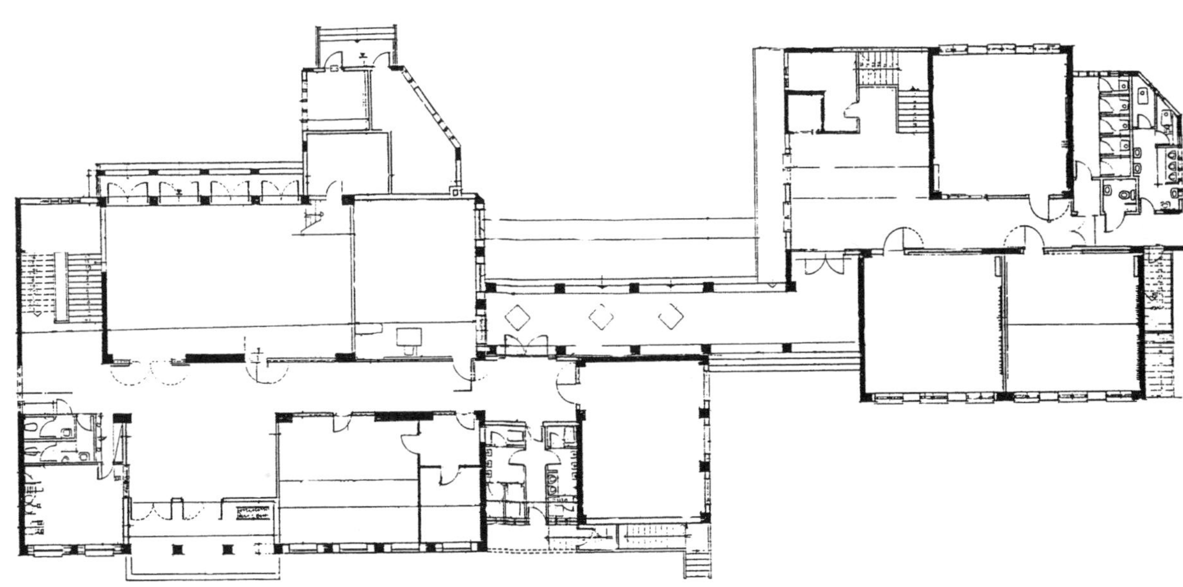

① *With attractive pink concrete walls, the school is built to be fire and earthquake resistant.*

② *Situated at the highest point of the site, the school affords views across the surrounding area.*

③ *View from one of the play areas.*

④ *Ground floor plan; the school is a series of linked two-storey elements.*

⑤ *The basketball court.*

⑥ *Main elevation.*

6

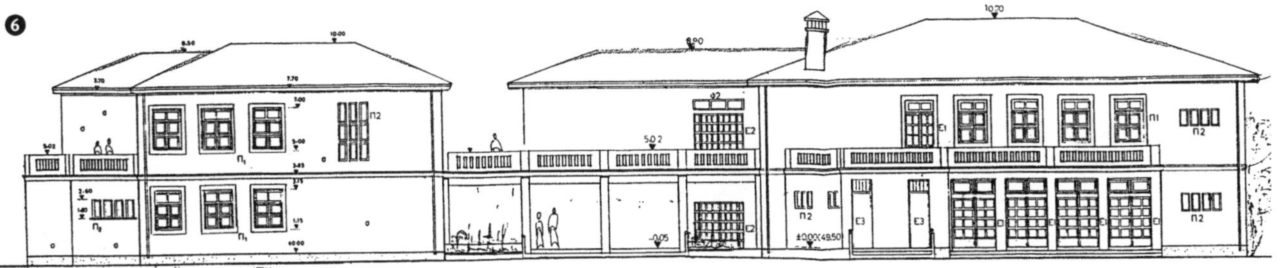

Appendices

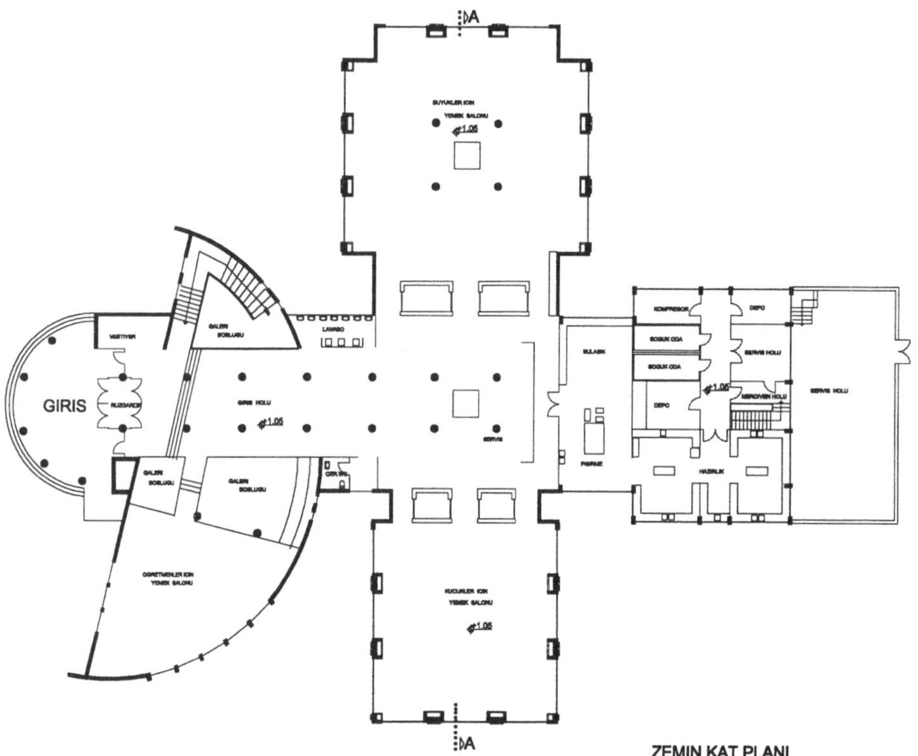
A
BUYUKLER ICIN
YEMEK SALONU
+1.05
GALERI
BOSLUGU
LAVABO
VESTIYER
GIRIS
GIRIS HOLU
+1.05
SERVIS
GALERI
BOSLUGU
GALERI
BOSLUGU
OGRETMENLER ICIN
YEMEK SALONU
KUCUKLER ICIN
YEMEK SALONU
+1.05
KOMPRESOR
DEPO
SOGUK ODA
SOGUK ODA
SERVIS HOLU
BULASIK
DEPO
+1.05
MERDIVEN HOLU
SERVIS HOLU
HAZIRLIK
A
ZEMIN KAT PLANI

The Turkish Basic Education Programme was submitted as an entry for this compendium but did not meet the criteria for inclusion. The PEB Steering Committee, nevertheless, agreed that the project deserved wider attention and decided to include it in this publication.

In August 1997, the Turkish government drew up legislation to pave the way for a massive expansion of the basic education system. Financed from general taxation, and with the support of national and international organisations, the programme is designed to generate a step change in enrolments and implement compulsory schooling for 6–14 year olds.

In the three years following the approval of legislation, there has been significant progress, with 20 000 new classrooms erected in 636 new schools. Additional new facilities are to follow, in the second and third phases of the programme. Their design conforms to the basic templates laid out in the Ministry for Education's *Standards Manual for School Buildings*, which sets minimum requirements with regard to equipment, furniture and materials.

Buildings are located in areas which are easily accessible to the whole community, and some facilities, such as libraries and sports halls, are available for community use out of school hours. Soundproof and fire resistant materials provide a pleasant and safe environment, with the vibrant colour scheme selected for its motivational qualities.

The guidelines make special provisions for the needs of students with physical disabilities, stipulating that high-rise structures should be avoided and setting a limit to the number of floors. Ease of access is further enhanced by locating classrooms for the early years pupils on the ground floor and building separate entrances for nursery and school children.

Designed to meet the needs of an evolving education system, the programme provides for widespread access to the latest information technology, both for staff and students. Computerised networks support all school administrative tasks. Computer and science laboratories are connected to the internet. Curricular software, currently in development, will be integrated into classroom teaching.

Although still in its early stages, the programme has already achieved impressive results within a very short space of time. Its success will be judged by its ability to extend the benefits of education beyond the primary age group, to parents, families and the wider community. When completed, it will serve as the foundation for a technologically sophisticated and widely accessible lifelong learning system.

For more information, contact:

A. Remzi Sezgin
Deputy Under-Secretary
Ministry of National Education
06548 Bakanliklar
Ankara, Turkey
Tel: 90 312 418 7650
Fax: 90 312 425 1724
Email: arsezgin@meb.gov.tr

2nd High School of Salamina
George Papandzeae, Hydzas 4, Salamina
GREECE 18900
Tel: 304677263

Allgemeinbildende Höhere Schule
Stift-Viktring-StraBe 25
Klagenfurt-Viktring
AUSTRIA 9073
Tel: 43463281469
Email: brg.viktring@Isr-ktn.gv.at

Allgemeinbildende Höhere Schule und Handelsakademie
Geringergasse
Vienna
AUSTRIA 1110
Tel: 4317679555202
Fax: 4317679555204
Email: pschleri@bhakwien11.at
Website: www.bhakwien11.at

Asqua-Centro di Educazione e Formazione Ambientale
Asqua-Cea Di Legambiente
Piazza Risorgimento, 16
Ponte a Poppi
ITALY 52013
Tel: 390575520462
Fax: 390575520463
Email: asqua@technet.it
Website: www.asqua.it

Cégep de Saint-Hyacinthe
3000 av. Boullé
Saint-Hyacinthe
CANADA J2S 1H9
Tel: 14507736800
Fax: 14507739971
Email: ggagne@cegepsth.qc.ca

Centre de formation du transport routier, Saint-Jérôme
17 000 rue Aubin
St-Janvier
Mirabel
CANADA J7J 1B1
Tel: 14504350167
Fax: 14504350933
Email: rochonb@csrdn.qc.ca

Chr. Hogeschool De Driestar
Postbus 368
Gouda
NETHERLANDS 2800 AJ
Tel: 31180540333
Fax: 31182538449

Collège l'Estaque
348 rue Rabelais
Marseilles
FRANCE 13016
Tel: 33495069320
Fax: 33495069321
Email: college-estaque.13@wanadoo.fr

Collège Victor Louis
52, avenue de Thouars
Talence
FRANCE 33405
Tel: 33557350060
Fax: 33557370061
Email: c.vlouis.talence@ac-bordeaux.fr
Website:
www.ac-bordeaux.fr/etablissement/VLouis/vlouis/index.htm

Complexo Escolar do Rodo
Quinta do Rodo
5050 Peso da Régua
PORTUGAL 5050
Tel: 351254322460
Fax: 35125425139

Corona Information Centre, University of Helsinki
Viikinkaari 11
Helsinki 71
FINLAND 00710
Tel: 35891911
Fax: 358919158011
Email: viikki-lib@helsinki.fi
Website: http://helsinki.fi/infokeskus/kirasto

Deachon High School
Jukjong-Dong 11
Boryong City
Chungchung Nam-Do
Boryong
KOREA 355-0120
Tel: 824529314362
Fax: 824529314374
Email: daechon@chungnam-o.ed.chungnam.kr

Dokuz Eylul University Foundation 75th Year Primary and Secondary School
Erdem Caddesi Buca
Izmir
TURKEY
Tel: 902324534155
Fax: 902324534156
Email: lcavas@hotmail.com
Website: www.ilk.deu.edu.tr

École communale fondamentale de Remicourt
Rue Jules Melotte,15
Remicourt
BELGIUM 4350
Tel: 3219545854

École Polymécanique de Laval
4095, Boulevard Lévesque Est
Laval
CANADA H7E 2R3
Tel: 14506618150
Fax: 14506618159
Email: polymecanique@cslaval.qc.ca
Website: www.cslaval.qc.ca/polymecanique

École Terre-Lune
Neyruz
SWITZERLAND 1740
Tel: 41263051256
Fax: 41263051214
Email: ducrotc@etatfr.ch

Engjaskoli District Primary School
Vallengi 14
Reykjavik
ICELAND 112
Tel: 3545101300
Fax: 3545101305
Email: engjask@isment.is
Website: http://rvikisment.is~engjask/

Escola Básica 1,2,3/JI de Vasco da Gama
Rua Ilha dos Amores- Parque Expo
Lisboa
PORTUGAL 1990
Tel: 351218930300
Fax: 351218930305

Escola Básica 3/ Secundária das Laranjeiras
Rue des Laranjeiras
Ponta Delgada
PORTUGAL 9500-317
Tel: 351296383920
Fax: 351296383851
Email: tesc0470@mail.telepac.pt
Website: www.esgb-laranjeiras.rects.pl

Escola de Ensino Básico 2,3 de Miragaia
Calcada Das Virtudes
Porto
PORTUGAL 4050
Tel: 351220306234
Fax: 35122030625

Escola EB 2,3 de Júlio Brandão
Rua Padre António José Carvalho Guimarães
Vila Nova de Famalicão
PORTUGAL 4760
Tel: 351252308220

Escola Profissional da Região Alentejo (EPRAL)
EPRAL- Fundacão Alentejo
Avenida Dinis Miranda No 116
Evora
PORTUGAL 7000-751
Tel: 351266759100
Fax: 351266743397
Email: epral@mail.telepac.pt
Website: www.epral.pt

Escuela Francisco Beltrán Otero
Limon S/N
Col. Ampliacion Los Nogales
Villa dé Garcia
Monterrey Nuevo Leon
MEXICO

Faculté d'aménagement, Université de Montréal
Direction des immeubles
C.P. 6128
Succursale Centre-ville
Montréal
CANADA H3C 3J7
Tel: 15143436242
Fax: 15143436604
Email: adamsru@di.umontreal.ca

Faculties of Law and Social and Economic Sciences
Universitätsstrasse 15
Graz
AUSTRIA 8010
Tel: 43316380
Fax: 433809820
Website: http://www.kfunigraz.ac.at/

Fenix Kunskapscentrum
Box 180
Vaggeryd
SWEDEN 56724
Tel: 4639378713
Fax: 4639378720
Email: fenix@vaggeryd.se
Website: www.fenix.vaggeryd.se

Ganztagsschule Schumpeterweg
Schumpeterweg-Kummergasse
Vienna
AUSTRIA 1210
Tel: 4312909754

Groupe scolaire Roger Gavage
90 rue des Prolières
Fontaines St. Martin
FRANCE 69270
Tel: 33478222239
Email: ecolerogergavage@wanadoo.fr

Haagse Hogeschool
Johanna Westerdijkplein 75
The Hague
NETHERLANDS 2521EN
Tel: 31704458888
Fax: 31704458805
Email: elzeb@cbh.hhs.nl
Website: www.hhs.nl

Heinävaara Elementary School
Heinävaaran ala-aste
Isäntäläntie 1
Kiihtelysvaara
FINLAND 82110
Tel: 35813717920

Höhere Technische Bundeslehranstalt
Thaliastrasse 125
Vienna
AUSTRIA 1160
Tel: 431491110
Fax: 43149111999
Email: direktion@htlw16.ac.at
Website: www.htlw16.ac.at

Húsaskóli Primary School
Dalhus 41
Reykjavik
ICELAND 112
Tel: 3545676100
Fax: 3545676556
Email: selma@ismennt.is
Website: www.ismennt.is/vefir/husask/

Institut des Hautes Études Commerciales de Liège
rue Louvrex, 14
Liège
BELGIUM 4000
Tel: 3242327222

Institut Supérieur des Beaux-Arts et Institut Supérieur d'Architecture Saint-Luc
26 Rue Sainte Marie
Liège
BELGIUM 4000
Tel: 3242223982
Fax: 3242233908

Instituto de Enseñanza Secundaria "Cardenal López Mendoza"
Plaza Doctor Albiñana, s/n
Burgos
SPAIN

Irmak School
Irmak Özel Ilkögretim Okulu
Cemil Topuzlu cad.
No:112
Caddebostan-Kadiköy
Istanbul
TURKEY 81060
Tel: 902164113923
Fax: 902164113926
Email: eyilmaz@irmak.k12.tr
Website: www.irmak.k12.tr

Istanbul Technical University – Dr. Sedat Üründül Nursery School
Istanbul Technical University
Ayazaga Campus
Istanbul
TURKEY 80626
Tel: 902122853333
Fax: 902122856610
Email: saglamer@itu.edu.tr
Website: www.itu.edu.tr

L'Autre École
1 Place Govaert
Commune D'Auderghem
Bruxelles
BELGIUM 1160
Tel: 3226607238
Email: lep@archuclac.be

La Trobe University
Bundoora
Victoria
AUSTRALIA 3083
Tel: 61394792077
Fax: 61394791559
Email: d.stephenson@latrobe.edu.au
Website: www.latrobe.edu.au

Laboratorio di Educazione Ambientale della Maremma Toscana – la Finoria
Via Monticello 66
Gavorrano
ITALY 58023
Tel: 39566846248
Fax: 39566844211
Email: lea@ouverture.it
Website: www.ouverture.it/lea/

Letterkenny Institute of Technology
Port Road
Letterkenny
County Donegal
IRELAND
Tel: 3537464100
Fax: 3537464111
Email: mary.daly@lyit.ie
Website: www.lyit.ie

Limerick Institute of Technology
Moylish Park
Limerick
IRELAND
Tel: 35361208208
Fax: 35361208209
Email: mcadm@lit.ie
Website: www.lit.ie

Lycée Léonard de Vinci
4, avenue Georges Pompidou
Levallois-Perret
FRANCE 92304
Tel: 33141051212
Fax: 33141051200
Website: www-ac-versailles-Fr/etabliss/lyc-vinci-levallois

Notley Green County Primary School
Blickling Road
Black Notley
Braintree
Essex
UNITED KINGDOM CM7 82J
Tel: 441376343485
Fax: 441376553894

Ranelagh Multi-Denominational School
Ranelagh Road
Dublin, 6
IRELAND
Tel: 35314961722
Fax: 35314961722

Rauma Teacher Training School
Seminaarinkatu 1
Rauma
FINLAND 26100
Tel: 358283780452
Fax: 358283780454
Email: eija.kajantola@utu.fi
Website: www.rnk.utu.fi

Sir John Colfox School
The Ridgeway
Bridgeport
UNITED KINGDOM DTE 3D7
Tel: 441308422291
Fax: 441308420036
Email: office@colfox.dorset.sch.uk

Soininen Primary School
Kenttapolku 3
Helsinki
FINLAND 00700
Tel: 358931080397
Fax: 358931080700

Staatliches Berufskolleg Glas – Keramik – Gestaltung des Landes Nordrhein-Westfalen
Zu den Fichten 19
Rheinbach
GERMANY 53359
Tel: 49222692200
Fax: 492226922020
Email: GFS@glasfachschule.de
Website: www.glasfachschule.de

Städtische Gesamtschule Barmen
Unterdörnen 1
Wuppertal
GERMANY 42283
Tel: 492025635115
Fax: 492025638174

Toga Elementary School/Lower Secondary School/ Community Centre
184 Toga
Toga-mura
Higashi-tonami-gun, Toyama-Pref
Toga-mura
JAPAN 939-2507
Tel: 81763682040 or 81763682151
Fax: 81763682062

Tomaree Education Centre
Salamander Way
Salamander Bay
New South Wales
AUSTRALIA 2317
Tel: 61249811595
Fax: 61249842275

University of Limerick, Library and Information Services Building
Plassey Campus
Limerick
IRELAND
Tel: 35361333644
Fax: 35361330316

Willow Tree Primary School
Arnold Road
Ealing
UNITED KINGDOM UB5 5EF
Tel: 442088454181
Fax: 442088452253
Email: dharvey@willow-tree.ealing.sch.uk

Yanominami Elementary School
4-17-1 Yano-minami
Aki-ku, Hiroshima-Pref
Hiroshima-City
JAPAN 736-0086
Tel: 81828886811
Fax: 81828886822

Cégep de Saint-Hyacinthe

ABCP Architecture et Urbanisme
1511, rue St Antoine
Saint-Hyacinthe
CANADA J25 3L5
Tel: 14507781151
Fax: 14507781594

Groupe scolaire Roger Gavage

Alain Chomel
Chomel Architectes
61, rue de la Part Dieu
Lyon
FRANCE 69003
Tel: 33478600366
Fax: 33478602126

Notley Green County Primary School

Allford Hall Monaghan Morris
Simon Allford
2nd Floor, Block B, 5–23 Old Street
London
UNITED KINGDOM EC1V 9HL
Tel: 442072515261
Fax: 442072515123
Email: info@ahmm.co.uk

Lycée Léonard de Vinci

André et Christian Roth
Agence d'architecture André et Christian ROTH
140, Route de Longpont
Ste Geneviève des Bois
FRANCE 91700
Tel: 33160157340
Fax: 33160157396
Email: A.ROTH@wanadoo.fr

Rauma Teacher Training School

Architects' office Laiho-Pulkkinen-Raunio
Mikko Pulkkinen
Kauppiaskatu 4B
Turku
FINLAND 20100
Tel: 35822777155
Fax: 35822777156
Email: mikko.pulkkinen@raksanet.fi

Allgemeinbildende Höhere Schule
und Handelsakademie

Architekten Nehrer + Medek und Partner
S. Bradic
Getreidemarkt 11
Vienna
AUSTRIA 1060
Tel: 4315815800
Fax: 431581580033
Email: Nehrer.Medek.Partner@chello.at

Höhere Technische Bundeslehranstalt

Architekten Nehrer + Medek und Partner
H. Pohl und W. Huber
Getreidemarkt 11
Vienna
AUSTRIA 1060
Tel: 4315815800
Fax: 431581580033
Email: Nehrer.Medek.Partner@chello.at

Chr. Hogeschool De Dreistar

Architektenbureau A.A Bos en Partners bv
P.A. Lenstra, ir.
Amalialaan 27
Baarn
NETHERLANDS 3743 KE
Tel: 31355416342
Fax: 31355413582
Email: info@bosenpartners.nl
Website: www.bosenpartners.nl

Collège Victor Louis

ARCOTEC
Alain Rodriguez
4, esplanade Charles de Gaulle
Pessac
FRANCE 33400
Tel: 33556467260
Fax: 33556467269
Email: ARCOTEC.AlainRODRIGUEZ@wanadoo.fr

Corona Information Centre,
University of Helsinki

ARK-House Architects Ltd
Hannu Huttunen, Markku Erholtz and Pentti Kareoja
Säästöpankinranta 8B
Helsinki
FINLAND 00530
Tel: 35897742480
Fax: 358977424888
Email: ark-house@megabaud.fi

Haagse Hogeschool

Atelier PRO
Hans van Beek and Leon Thier with
the cooperation of Rene Hoek
Kerkhoflaan 11A
Den Haag
NETHERLANDS 2585 JB
Tel: 31703506900
Fax: 31703514971
Email: info@atelierPRO.nl

Yanominami Elementary School

Atelier Zo
702 Sunny City Shinjuku Gyoen
2-1-3 Shinjuku
Shinjuku-ku
Tokyo
JAPAN 160-0022
Tel: 81352691581
Fax: 81352691583
Email: tokyo@zoz.co.jp

Institut des Hautes Études Commerciales de Liège

Bruno Albert and Camille Ghysen
Bruno Albert Architecte et Associés S.C.
Rue Mont Saint-Martin, nº 7
Liège
BELGIUM 4000
Tel: 3242236356
Fax: 3242229016
Email: bruno.albert@skynet.be

Escuela Francisco Beltrán Otero

C.A.P.F.C.E.
(Comité del Programa Federal de Construcción de Escuelas)
Vito Alessio Robles #380
Colonia Florida
Mexico, D.F.
MEXICO 01030
Tel: 5255546798
Fax: 5254804722
Email: federal@capfce.gob.mx

École communale fondamentale
de Remicourt

Carine Driesmans and Marc Zweber
Formes et Espaces, Atelier d'architecture
Société interprofessionnelle d'architectes
route des Chantoirs, 25
Aywaille
BELGIUM 4920
Tel: 3243608337
Fax: 3243609892
Email: formes.espaces@skynet.be
Website: http://users.skynet.be/formes.espaces

Deachon High School

Chan Young Park
Jung-Ju Architectural Firm
Sunhwa Dong 382–80
Jung-Gu
Deajun
KOREA 301-050
Tel: 82422545318
Email: ja5318@chollian.net

Laboratorio di Educazione Ambientale
della Maremma Toscana – la Finoria

Claudio Sargosa
Via Bicocchi 66
58022 Folonica (Gr) Via G. Pascoli Nr. 5
Firenze
ITALY 50100
Tel: 390555520544
Fax: 390555520544
Email: saragosa@unifi.it

Heinävaara Elementary School

Cuningham Group
201 Main Street SE
Suite 325
Minneapolis, MN
UNITED STATES 55416
Tel: 16123793400
Fax: 16123794400
Email: jhoskens@cuningham.com
Website: www.cuningham.com

Cégep de Saint-Hyacinthe

Duclos Fournier, architectes
675, ave. Sainte Marie
Saint-Hyacinthe
CANADA J2S 4R8
Tel: 14507734431
Fax: 14507737731
Email: architectes@duclosfournier.qc.ca

Institut Supérieur des Beaux-Arts et Institut Supérieur d'Architecture Saint-Luc

Eugène Moureau
a.u.s.e
9, Boulevard Frère Orban
Liège
BELGIUM 4000
Tel: 3242229050
Fax: 3242237178
Email: groupeause@yahoo.fr

Toga Elementary School/Lower Secondary School/Community Centre

Fabrica Artis Architects
Masato Fujino
1-4-9-101 Kita-Shinjuku
Shinjuku-ku
Tokyo
JAPAN 169-0074
Tel: 81353323320
Fax: 81353323321
Email: YQW10616@nifty.ne.jp

Escola Profissional da Região Alentejo (EPRAL)

Francisco da Silva Dias
HCI, Construções S.A.
Avenida Almirante Gago Coutinho, nº 131
Lisboa
PORTUGAL 1700-029
Tel: 351218421200
Fax: 351218483024
Email: hci@netc.pt

Allgemeinbildende Höhere Schule

Gernot Kulterer
Klopstockstrasse 3
Villach
AUSTRIA 9500
Tel: 43424222578
Fax: 434242225784

Húsaskóli Primary School

Gudmundur Gunnarsson
Gunnarsson and Ivarsson Arkitektathjónustan s.f.
Hverfisgata 26
Reykjavík
ICELAND 101
Tel: 3545625020
Email: gudmundur@arkitektur.is
Website: www.arkitektur.is

Istanbul Technical University - Dr. Sedat Üründül Nursery School

Gülsün Saglamer and Meltem Aksoy
Istanbul Technical University
Ayazaga Campus
Rector's Office
Istanbul
TURKEY 80626
Tel: 902122853333
Fax: 902122856610
Email: saglamer@itu.edu.tr

Faculties of Law and
Social and Economic Sciences

Günther Domenig and Hermann Eisenköck
Architects Domenig/Eisenköck
Jahngasse 9/1
Graz
AUSTRIA 8010
Tel: 43316827753
Fax: 433168277539
Email: office@domenig.at
Website: www.domenig.at

Soininen Primary School

Ilmari Lahdelma
Lahdelma & Mahlamäki Architecture Office
Tehtaankatu 29 A
Helsinki
FINLAND 00150
Tel: 358096213033
Fax: 358096213155
Email: ilmari.lahdelma@ark-l-m.fi
Website: www.arc-lahdelmamahlamaki.com

École Terre-Lune

ITIS Architectes Sàrl
A. Cascione, Cl. Chassot, L.H. Clément et P. Clozza
Av. de l'Europe 8
Fribourg
SWITZERLAND 1700
Tel: 41263232109
Fax: 41263233741
Email: itis.architectes@bluewin.ch

Fenix Kunskapscentrum

Jack Pattisson
j. j. pattison arkitekt
Skogslund
Ströby
Vislanda
SWEDEN 340 30
Tel: 4647230805
Fax: 4647230381
Email: jack.pattison@mailbox.calypso.net

Collège l'Estaque

Jacques Fradin and Jean-Michel Weck
Atelier d'Architecture
70, Cours Gambetta
Aix en Provence
FRANCE 13100
Tel: 33442174444
Fax: 33442174440
Email: fradin.weck@wanadoo.fr

Centre de formation du
transport routier, Saint-Jérôme

Jean-Marc Coursol
Consortium Coursol, Tremblay, L'Écuyer, Brisson, Poulin,
Villeneuve architectes
18 086, Charles street
St-Janvier
CANADA J7J 1C5
Tel: 14504308777
Fax: 14504351521
Email: j.m.c@videotron.ca

Letterkenny Institute of Technology

Jim Coady & Associates
Trinity House
Charleston Road
Ranelagh
Dublin 6
IRELAND
Tel: 35314976766
Fax: 35314970927
Email: admin@jim-coady.ie

Escola Básica 1,2,3/JI de Vasco da Gama

João Alfonso Pancada Correia and
Maria Otília Mesquita Nabais Ribeiro Santos
Direcção Regional de Educação de Lisboa
Praça de Alvalade nº 12 e 13
Lisboa
PORTUGAL 1749-070
Tel: 351218433900
Fax: 351218479885
Email: jose.revez@drel.min-edu.pt
Website: www.drel.min-edu.pt

Escola Básica 3/ Secundária das Laranjeiras

Jorge Manuel Farelo Pinto
J. Farelo Pinto-Gabinete de Arquitectura
Lda.
Rua 4 de Infantaria, 40 - R/C Dtº
Lisboa
PORTUGAL 1350-273
Tel: 351213875945 or 351213830681
Fax: 351213877200
Email: farelopinto@ip.pt

Instituto de Enseñanza Secundaria
"Cardenal López Mendoza"

Jose Antonio Gil-Fournier Carazo
C/ San Juan 34-1º -B
Burgos
SPAIN 09004
Tel: 34947205544
Fax: 34947205544
Email: grcarazo@ubu.es

Escola EB 2,3 de Júlio Brandão

José Manuel da Silva Vieira Coelho
DREN
Rua António Carneiro, 8
Porto
PORTUGAL 4349-003
Tel: 351225191100
Fax: 351225103151
Email: dren@dren.min-edu.pt

Escola de Ensino Básico 2,3 de Miragaia

José Miguel Regueiras
José Miguel Regueiras Arquitecto
R. Santos Pousada, 1252, 1º Dto
Porto
PORTUGAL 4000-483
Tel: 351225029184
Fax: 351225029184
Email: j.miguel.regueiras@clix.pt

Limerick Institute of Technology
University of Limerick, Library
and Information Services Building

Murray O'Laoire Architects
Merriman House
Brian Merriman Place
Lock Quay
Limerick
IRELAND
Tel: 35361316400
Fax: 35361316853
Email: mail@limerick.murrayolaoire.com
Website: www.murrayolaoire.com

Irmak School, Block B, Block C

Nevzat Sayin
Nevzat Sayin Mimarlik Hizmetleri Limited Sirketi
Icadiye Cad. No. 99, Kuzguncuk
81200 Istanbul
TURKEY
Tel: 902163100870
Fax: 902163100870
Email: nevsayin@notone.com.tr

Tomaree Education Centre

NSW Department of Public Works and Services
Stewart Morgan, Building Design Group
2–24 Rawson Place
Sydney
AUSTRALIA NSW 2000
Tel: 61293728342
Fax: 61293728399
Email: stewart.morgan@dpws.nsw.gov.au
Website: www.dpws.nsw.gov.au

Ranelagh Multi-Denominational School

O'Donnell and Tuomey Architects
20a Camden Row
Dublin 8
IRELAND
Tel: 35314752500
Fax: 35314751479
Email: info@odonnell-tuomey.ie

Dokuz Eylul University Foundation
75th Year Primary and Secondary School

Orcan Gündüz
Mustafa Düzgün, Göksel Sezer, Bahadir Yaldiz, Itir Erküçük
Dokuz Eylul University Faculty of Architecture
Sehitler Caddesi No:12, Alsancak
Izmir
TURKEY 35230
Tel: 902324640500
Fax: 902324648063
Email: orcan.gündüz@deu.edu.tr

Staatliches Berufskolleg Glas – Keramik –
Gestaltung des Landes Nordrhein-Westfalen

Parade Architekten
Christoph Parade, Brigitte Parade-Reese and Helmut Kühn
Saarwerdenstr 8
Düsseldorf
GERMANY 40547
Tel: 49211954960
Fax: 492119549611
Email: parade-architekten@t-online.de

Städtische Gesamtschule Barmen

Parade Architekten
Christoph Parade and Helmut Kühn
Saarwerdenstr 8
Düsseldorf
GERMANY 40547
Tel: 49211954960
Fax: 492119549611
Email: parade-architekten@t-online.de

Asqua – Centro di Educazione e
Formazione Ambientale

Roberto Mariottini and Michele Mariottini
Studio RM Mariottini Arch. Roberto
Via Dovizi, 2
Bibbiena (AR)
ITALY 52011
Tel: 390575536340
Fax: 390575539856
Email: RMstudio@technet.it

Complexo Escolar do Rodo

Rosa Bela Costa and Luis Cunha
Ministério da Educaçao - DGAE
Av. 24 de Julho, 142 - 2º
Lisboa
PORTUGAL 1399-024
Tel: 3512139386478
Fax: 351213973082
Website: www.DGAE.Min-EDU.pt

Université de Montréal,
Faculté d'aménagement

Saucier + Perrotte/Menkès Shooner Dagenais
Anik Shooner/Gilles Saucier
5334, Boulevard Saint-Laurent
Montreal
CANADA H2T 1S1
Tel: 15142731700
Fax: 15142733501
Email: spa@saucierperrotte.com
Website: www.saucierperrotte.com

2nd High School of Salamina

School Building Organisation S.A.
Evangelia Tsatsou
30 Favierou Street
Athens
GREECE 104 38
Tel: 3015220735
Fax: 3015220246

Ganztagsschule Schumpeterweg

Stefan K. Hübner with Peter Leibetseder
Strohgasse 18
Vienna
AUSTRIA 1030
Tel: 43171432820
Fax: 431714328219
Email: arch.huebner@vienna.at

Húsakóli Primary School

Sveinn Ivarsson

Sveinn Ivarsson aGf. and arkitektur.ls.ehf
Lyngháls 3
Reykjavik
ICELAND 110
Tel: 3545679006
Email: ivarsson@islandia.is
Email: ysaglikova@süperonline.com

Sir John Colfox School

Terence O'Rourke plc

Jane Lock-Smith
Everdene House
Wessex Fields
Deansleigh Road
Bournemouth, Dorset
UNITED KINGDOM BH7 7DU
Tel: 441202421142
Fax: 441202430055
Email: maildesk@torplc.com

Willow Tree Primary School

Unicorn Consultancy Services (in succession to BRETS)

Zbigniew M. Behnke
1st Floor, 22-24 Uxbridge Road
Ealing
London
UNITED KINGDOM W5 2BP
Tel: 442087585870
Fax: 442087585822
Email: behnkez@unicorn-cs.co.uk
Website: www.unicornworks.co.uk

Engjaskoli District Primary School

Uti og Inni, architects

Baldur O. Svavarsson/Jon Thor Thorvaldsson
Thingholtsstraeti 27
Reykjavik
ICELAND 101
Tel: 3545527660
Fax: 3545527661
Email: uti.inni@arkitekt.is
Website: www.uti.inni.is

École Polymécanique de Laval

Viau Bergeron Architectes

Claude Bergeron
3285, boul. St-Martin est
bureau 201
Laval
CANADA H7E 4T6
Tel: 14506618427
Fax: 14506612149
Email: viau.bergeron.architectes@qc.aira.com

Irmak School, Block A

Yildirim Saglikova

Yildirim Saglikova Mimarlik Muhendislik Müsavirlik Hizmetleri
Limited Sirketi
Zambakli Sokak No.12
3. Levent
Istanbul
TURKEY 80620
Tel: 902122810712
Fax: 902122812898

La Trobe University

Yunken Freeman Architects

Roy McCowan Simpson (deceased)
AUSTRALIA

L'Autre École

Yves A. Lepère and Frédéric Andrieux

Sites & Cites
2é, rue Chapelle Sainte Anne
Walhain-Saint-Paul
BELGIUM 1457
Tel: 3210655370
Fax: 3210658513
Email: lepere@arch.ucl.ac.be

PEB Themes

Work area A:
The school of the future

Category A1: ***Schools in the information society*** — School facilities, including documentation and resource centres, whose design is adapted for the educational use of information and communication technology.

Category A2: ***Facilities which provide for lifelong learning in the community*** (including adult learning, training for business and industry, child care and pre-school provision, and other human services), and those which benefit from new partnerships and new funding arrangements.

Category A3: ***Educational facilities and the environment*** — Facilities which make use of choice materials, energy-saving systems, siting or management in a safe and environmentally friendly way, or school grounds which promote environmental education.

Work area B:
Tertiary education: coping with demand

Category B1: ***Libraries and learning resource centres*** for tertiary education which meet the evolving needs of staff and students in new ways, in response to the impact of technology on teaching and learning and the growth of distance learning.

Category B2: ***Design of institutions for the early years of tertiary education*** — Facilities appropriately designed to provide for increased numbers of students and growing diversity in course content and structure.

Work area C:
Strategies for managing the educational infrastructure

Category C1: ***Maintenance*** — Facilities which are effectively maintained or which have been brought up to the standard necessary for education in the twenty-first century.

Category C2: ***Space management and use in large institutions*** — Large secondary schools and tertiary institutions which demonstrate efficient management and use of space.

Category C3: ***Institutions which have used alternative ways of financing capital expenditure,*** including the use of private financing.

Category C4: ***Health, safety and security*** — Facilities which provide so far as possible for safety from natural disaster or accidental or deliberate acts of man, through the use of particular construction materials and attention to standards, design, building management and risk assessement (areas of concern include fire prevention, earthquake and disaster management, the quality of the indoor environment, traffic management, controlling hazardous substances, and personal and material security).

Schools in the information society – A1

Lifelong learning in the community – A2

Educational facilities and the environment – A3

Libraries and learning resource centres – B1

Design for early years of tertiary education – B2

Maintenance – C1

Space management and use in large institutions – C2

Financing capital expenditure – C3

Health, safety and security – C4

OECD PUBLICATIONS, 2, rue André-Pascal, 75775 PARIS CEDEX 16
PRINTED IN FRANCE
(95 2001 01 1 P) ISBN 92-64-18613-1 – No. 51589 2001